Black Boys Burning

BLACK BOYS BURNING

The 1959 Fire at the
Arkansas Negro Boys
Industrial School

Grif Stockley

University Press of Mississippi / Jackson

www.upress.state.ms.us

The University Press of Mississippi is a member
of the Association of American University Presses.

First printing 2017

∞

Portions of this work previously appeared in "The Twenty-One Deaths
Caused by the 1959 Fire at the Arkansas Negro Boys Industrial School:
An Isolated Case of 'Neglect' or an Instance of Racial Violence?" In
Race and Ethnicity in Arkansas: New Perspectives, edited by John A.
Kirk, 71–81. Fayetteville: University of Arkansas Press, 2014.

Library of Congress Cataloging-in-Publication Data

Names: Stockley, Grif, author.
Title: Black boys burning : the 1959 fire at the Arkansas Negro Boys
Industrial School / Grif Stockley.
Description: Jackson : University Press of Mississippi, [2017] | Includes
bibliographical references and index.
Identifiers: LCCN 2017007287 (print) | LCCN 2017011099 (ebook) | ISBN
9781496812698 (hardcover : alk. paper) | ISBN 9781496812704 (epub single)
| ISBN 9781496812711 (epub institutional) | ISBN 9781496812728 (pdf
single) | ISBN 9781496812735 (pdf institutional)
Subjects: LCSH: Arkansas Negro Boys Industrial School (Wrightsville,
Ark.)—Fire, 1959. | Race discrimination—Arkansas—History—20th century.
| Juvenile justice, Administration of—Arkansas—History—20th century. |
Segregation in education—Arkansas—History—20th century.
Classification: LCC HV9105.A82 S76 2017 (print) | LCC HV9105.A82 (ebook) |
DDC 365/.976773—dc23
LC record available at https://lccn.loc.gov/2017007287

British Library Cataloging-in-Publication Data available

To my sisters,
Harriet and Sally,
and in memory of my brother-in-law,
Carlos Lopez

Contents

Acknowledgments

I wish to acknowledge the generous help of the North Little Rock Laman Library. It was a source of great pride to be selected as a recipient in 2010 of a writing fellowship sponsored by that institution.

Some people (but certainly not all) met my efforts to research the history of the school and the events surrounding the fire with great reluctance and refused to discuss it. Understandably, a number of people preferred not to be reminded of their association with that institution. Those who were willing to share their memories and provide assistance I thank profusely. I take this opportunity to express my deep appreciation to the Frank Lawrence family of North Little Rock, and I would be remiss if I didn't explain its contribution. It was Lindsey Cross's brother, Frank Lawrence, who raised the many questions about the fire and the deaths of the boys that have long been unasked and unanswered during his efforts to make a documentary film. I would learn that Lawrence had done important research on the story of the fire until his financial resources were exhausted and his efforts to gain outside support for the project failed. As I acknowledge throughout the text and endnotes, his interviews with former inmates, family members of survivors, employees, and others have brought to light relevant and significant information. He arranged for me to talk with his family members, former inmates, and employees as well as sharing the numerous filmed interviews he had conducted. Additionally, he sat for an extended interview while I was an employee at the Butler Center for Arkansas Studies, which is now archived in the center's audio/visual project.

Our interpretations and conclusions of the events are sometimes different. But had Frank Lawrence not insisted that the deaths of the boys be remembered, the fiftieth anniversary of the fire would have gone unnoticed.

Guy Lancaster, editor of the online Encyclopedia of Arkansas History and Culture, read drafts and made helpful suggestions. EOA has become an invaluable resource to the entire country and not infrequently the world. I thank my sister Sally Johnson for her editorial suggestions. I thank Roy Reed, whose biography of Orval Faubus was selected as a 1997 New York Times Notable Book and is the definitive work on that complex individual, for his careful reading of the final draft and suggestions. No book on history can be written without the assistance of librarians, and I especially thank Geoffery Stark, Special Collections at the University of Arkansas (Fayetteville), for his relentless searching of the Orval Faubus Papers. I also thank Brady Banta, Malissa Davis, and the Special Collections staffs at Arkansas State University, Linda Pine and the University of Arkansas at Little Rock, Jimmy Bryant and the staff of Special Collections at the University of Central Arkansas, and the staff of the Arkansas State Archives. I also wish to thank Bobby Roberts and David Stricklin and the Central Arkansas Library System for their support of the Ruled by Race Project that made possible my employment at the Butler Center for Arkansas Studies while a part of the research on the history of the Negro Boys Industrial School was being conducted. I thank Craig Gill, Emily Bandy, Katie Keene, Valerie Jones, Todd Lape, and others at the University Press of Mississippi for bringing this book to publication.

It pleases me to note that not all the research was a grim affair. I was graciously permitted to attend a reunion in Los Angeles of members of the family of Tandy Washington Coggs, the first and best superintendent of the Negro Boys Industrial School. My interviews with Dr. Granville Coggs and members of the Coggs family were a delight. I also thank Tom Dillard, Dorothy Mattison, Joyce Williams, Howard Lee Nash, Gina Reynolds, Octavia Hill, Lorraine Smith, Erin Tulk, SiKia Brown, Teresa Marks, Joyce Elliott, Bob Razer, Leslie Peacock, Wanda Gray, Moira Bryant, Jo Blatti, Steve

Copley, Rhonda Stewart, Linda McDowell, and Danyelle McNeil. I thank Michael Levine for his superb copyediting. As always, I thank Lynn Pence for her infinite patience and assistance.

Introduction: The Fire This Time

After the passage of voting restrictions in the 1890s, school boards
had lost all political motivation to fund black public education; they
needed only to maintain the appearance of black public schooling as
a precaution against the unlikely event of federal intervention.

—**Story L. Matkin-Rawn**, "'We Fight for the Rights of
Our Race': Black Arkansans in the Era of Jim Crow"

In an editorial on March 20, 1959, L. C. Bates, the African American publisher of the *Arkansas State Press*, wrote the following: "We
wonder if the white man in the South who has set the pattern for
the Negro to live by can find any consolation for the irreparable
damage that his system has caused."[1] Fifteen days prior, an early
morning fire had burned to death twenty-one African American
adolescents who were locked inside a dormitory at the Arkansas
Negro Boys School outside of Little Rock. No employee was present to unlock the door. On March 9, nine black school children in
Georgia had drowned when a bus transporting them to a segregated school overturned. As L. C. and his wife Daisy Bates knew
only too well,[2] white supremacy had been carried out by slavery,
"bad science," murder, rape, terrorism, lynching, massacres, mass
incarceration, peonage, disfranchisement, racial cleansing, arson,
racial covenants, predatory lending, loan discrimination, redlining,
blockbusting, segregation, intimidation, humiliation, discrimination, denial of free speech, termination from employment, a truly
massive theft of financial resources for services lawfully intended
for black citizens, quarantine rather than effective treatment of
black persons diagnosed with tuberculosis, paternalism, and a civil

and criminal justice system that routinely denied African Americans due process and equal protection of the law.[3]

As an integral part of impediments to African America rights, the official and unofficial writing of the South's racial past sometimes resembled propaganda rather than history in order to justify the actions of white southerners.[4] Notwithstanding the carnage and devastation caused by the Civil War, accounts of the South's struggle and its defeat over time have often been transformed into an occasion for nostalgia, reenactments, and "legends" rather than attempts to come to terms with its actual history.[5]

Had they been so inclined, however, the fire at the Arkansas Negro Boys Industrial School and its history could have squarely given southerners the motivation to investigate their actual record of providing "separate but equal institutions." Coming on the heels of the Little Rock Central High School desegregation crisis in 1957, with its shocking articles and photographs sent all over the world of nine black children and newsmen being cursed and assaulted by a white mob, the circumstances of the deaths of the boys eighteen months later was once again an embarrassment to the state.

A number of investigations concerning the fire would begin almost immediately under the direction of Governor Orval Faubus, under whose thumb was the state police, the state fire marshal, and the board of the Negro Boys Industrial School (NBIS) (1931–1968), which oversaw the school. The efforts on the part of the white power structure in Little Rock to control the conclusions reached about the conditions and the deaths of the boys and the attempted pushback by blacks themselves during this crisis explain much about how white supremacy was managed over the duration of the NBIS. Among the conclusions of the grand jury was a moral indictment of the Arkansas legislature, "who should have been ashamed" for having permitted the transparently egregious conditions at the school at Wrightsville and the "people of Arkansas who did nothing about [them]." Having tiptoed up to the line of acknowledging the consequences of systematic racism, the white power structure implied its behavior was an anomaly. To attribute any "irreparable damage" to white supremacy would have opened up the entire behavior of white southerners for debate.

Significantly, the history of the Negro Boys Industrial School and the investigations and conclusions reached by the various institutions and bodies surrounding the deaths of the boys present an opportunity to analyze this era from a standpoint other than the Little Rock Central High School desegregation crisis in 1957, which has become a cottage industry for scholars. As useful as that perspective continues to be, the initial desegregation at Central High mostly involved middle-class students who had been carefully vetted. In fact, overwhelmingly, black Arkansans in Little Rock during the era of the fire worked at low wage jobs and were mired in poverty. While wealthy and/or influential families sometimes have avoided prosecution or incarceration in inferior facilities for their children through admission to private treatment options, poor black families were without the resources to privatize their problems (criminal and civil); it was the sons of those families who would be incarcerated in the Negro Boys Industrial School.

The intention to maintain white supremacy was what united white Arkansans during the era of the Negro Boys Industrial School, a period that encompasses and overlaps the 1957 Little Rock Central High Crisis. The paramount issue in 1957 was how to manage white supremacy, not whether to abolish it. Whatever the differences within the white community, there was no question about which race would remain in control politically and set the table for interaction between blacks and whites. Before, during, and after the abolishment of the Arkansas Negro Boys Industrial School, the eleven states that once composed the Old Confederacy operated not as representative democracies but rather as one-party states ruled by white males (the "solid South") whose most important order of business, privately and publicly, was very often to control and manage the black populations within their jurisdictions.

What can the history of this period of white supremacy and the history of the Arkansas Negro Boys Industrial School teach us? Were the deaths of the boys an isolated instance of criminal negligence on the part of the black superintendent or "someone" at the school as argued by Governor Faubus? Or can the deaths be attributed at least in part to the ostensibly irreparable damage caused by the relentless imposition of a system designed to advantage whites and control blacks? A careful telling of the history of the Arkansas Negro Boys Industrial School suggests that it is possible to begin to gain a fresh appreciation of the broader implications of the consequences of white supremacy. But so long as we continue to ignore the ripple effects of the damage caused by our unwillingness to confront our past, we will never understand the present.

Black Boys Burning

CHAPTER ONE

The Charred Remains of Children

Approximately 4 A.M., March 5, 1959, Wrightsville, Arkansas

Though the forecast for March 5, 1959, called for the temperature to warm up to nearly 60 degrees by the afternoon, the morning was cold and wet in central Arkansas. For two hours, thunderstorms had lashed the Wrightsville area, a sparsely populated, mostly black community twelve miles south of Little Rock on US Highway 65. Two miles to the east at the end of a dirt road stood the thirty or so buildings that made up the Negro Boys Industrial School, whose residents, fourteen and older, spent much of their time doing farm labor. By 4 a.m., the storms had tapered off to a light rain, lasting another forty minutes.

Inside the older boys' dormitory at Wrightsville, the only warmth was provided by a makeshift wood-burning stove fashioned from an oil drum. There was no heat coming from it when sixteen-year-old Arthur Ray Poole woke up about four a.m., smelling smoke. Around him in double-bunk beds separated by three feet from each other were sixty-eight other boys. Poole was one of two "sergeants." Charged with getting the boys up in the morning and turning off the lights at ten, sergeants were not entrusted with keys. In the darkness, he asked "someone if the wood heater had been lit." The answer came back, "No." It was then Poole saw the fire sweeping against the ceiling.

3

Like a number of the other boys confined at the Arkansas Negro Boys Industrial School, it was not the first time Poole, who was from Fort Smith on the border with Oklahoma, had been committed by juvenile court order to Wrightsville. He and O. F. "Charley" Meadows, the other "sergeant," began waking up the other boys. Complete hysteria was only seconds away as fire and smoke began to envelop the dormitory.[1]

Poole "started yelling and ran over to a window" to save himself. "Heavy gauge wire mesh" covered each of the sixteen windows, and some were more securely fastened than others. "Then I saw Charley the night sergeant had managed to get one of the window coverings off, so I got out through that window. As I climbed out that window, I saw several other kids fighting each other to get out the windows. There was a whole lot of screaming and shouting."[2] Telling his story to newsmen that morning, he added details that were repeated in similar accounts. "Four or five boys would all try to get through the same window at once. They were all screaming at each other. At another window, four boys were hitting the window covering with a chair trying to get it off." Arthur Ray admitted that he was part of the struggle: "I had to fight to get out the window."[3]

Charley Meadows told newsmen, "We did have a hard time in hammering off screens, but somehow we did. Then there was another rush, all trying to get out at once." Once a screen was pounded off, it was the survival of the fittest, in this case fittest meaning the biggest and strongest boys. But surviving also required luck because only two of the mesh coverings could be dislodged before the fire caught up with the boys who had not gotten through a window.

Again and again the survivors told the same story: "We all was trying to get out at the same time," fifteen-year-old Otis Sidney said, echoing Arthur Ray Poole. "Four or five boys would try to get out each window at one time. They just couldn't do it, and those waiting to get out kept pushing and shoving us. I know three boys who got badly burned before they could get out." Sidney reported that a group of about fifteen were caught by the fire in the northeast corner as they "were trying to 'beat the wire off' a window there."[4]

Robert Ramon, age fifteen, woke to a room filled by smoke and "boys screaming." He said, "The only thing I could think of was how to get out of there. I ran toward the window screen nearest my bed and kicked out the screen and left."[5]

Fifteen year-old Robert Paterson told UPI reporter Bernie Brown, "They just fought something terrible to get out of the window." Crying as he talked, he said, "Someone pushed me down. Somehow I got up and crawled out the window."

Nolan Fortner, whose age also was given as fifteen, told the same UPI reporter that he was awakened by the screaming. "The room was filled with smoke. I could hardly see. Everybody was trying to get out through the windows. I pushed one boy aside and crawled out."[6]

It is this brutal yet innocent candor that distinguishes these personal and brief accounts of the survivors' sheer terror. Their descriptions are the most realistic and believable, if partial, snapshot of what it was like inside the dormitory during the fire.[7]

Besides these published accounts, all other facts are still in dispute about what happened and why and their significance, that is, except for a single fact. The doors that possibly would have allowed the boys to escape death or injury were locked from the outside. P. R. Banks, whose job it was to be present with the boys at night and to unlock the doors in case of an emergency, was ill and had been hospitalized since February 20.[8]

These statements would not be the only accounts of what occurred inside and outside the dormitory. For example, Roy Davis, from Little Rock, would claim decades after the event that he had gotten out a window but climbed back inside to lead two other boys to safety.[9]

But this would have been impossible, according to James Watson, whose interview I recorded and transcribed in 2011 shortly before his death from cancer:

GS. Did you know of anybody [who] tried to go back in and help others?

JW. You couldn't. It was too dense. The fire and the smoke. You couldn't go back in unless you wanted to commit suicide.

When told that Roy Davis had said he had gone back inside and led two boys out, Mr. Watson, who remembered Davis, and described him as "everyday people," replied emphatically, *"No! That wasn't true. No, nobody went back in there. The building was already on fire."*

GS. Just telling you what he said.

JW. That's false there.

Mr. Watson had explained earlier:

When we got out, we thought everybody was getting out. You know, we heard screaming and hollering, so we started telling them to come on this side from the other side, you know, but they couldn't hear us. They couldn't hear us because they were so busy screaming and hollering, too, you know, so we went around the other side but they were in a corner, and we tried to pry [unintelligible] the screen loose, but the stick would break, and you couldn't get no grip there.[10]

Mr. Watson's account of the futile efforts of those outside to save anyone in the building was corroborated by Arthur Ray Poole, who had told newsmen, "After we got outside a bunch of us started yelling to the others the way to get out, but there was so much smoke and everything by that time that I guess they didn't hear us."

The fire was reported by telephone from Superintendent Lester Gaines's house not to the Little Rock Fire Department but to the offices of the Arkansas State Police, which, in turn, called the Pulaski County sheriff's department. The jailer on duty, Sid Sebastian, phoned the Little Rock Fire Department. The call was logged in at 4:30 a.m. Since the fire occurred outside the city, it took another call to Little Rock City Manager Dean Dauley to get permission to send a truck from station 13 on east Roosevelt to the scene.[11]

Arriving at the school, the firemen found no hydrants and laid six hundred feet of hose from the boys' swimming pool to the burning dormitory. It was harder than it looked. A muddy, open field separated the pool from the dormitory. Fireman Billy Griggo slipped on the wet earth, injuring his back. Survivors assisted firemen in putting down sixty feet of lumber across the muddy ground in order to get the truck in position to pump water, but according to fire captain W. A. Seaton, it was already too late by then. He told reporters that "the building was nearly gone when they arrived." His log entries state the cause of fire was "unknown."

Twenty-one boys died in the fire. Forty-eight survived.

The official ultimately responsible for the investigation of the fire was State Fire Marshal W. C. Struebing. Sounding more independent than it was, Struebing's position was that of an employee of the Arkansas State Police, an organization tightly under the control of the sitting governor. In trying to determine the cause of the blaze on the day of the fire, Lieutenant Struebing's job was complicated by the intense heat. He told the press the next day that "the ruins were too hot yesterday to investigate thoroughly, but, we have a crew conducting a more complete investigation today. It looks like an electrical fire."[12] Measured by loss of life, it was the worst fire in the state's history, a record that stood until 1965, when fifty-three workers at a Titan II missile installation were burned to death near Damascus in north-central Arkansas.

In its initial coverage on March 6, the *Arkansas Gazette* provided its readers a diagram of the destroyed edifice complete with measurements of the building and location of the bodies inside the older boys' dormitory (see Figure 1). Running north to south, the "entire front" of the "U" shaped building measured "114 by 30" and was used for various purposes, including a "chapel or classroom." The two wings on each end extended east for ninety-one feet. The

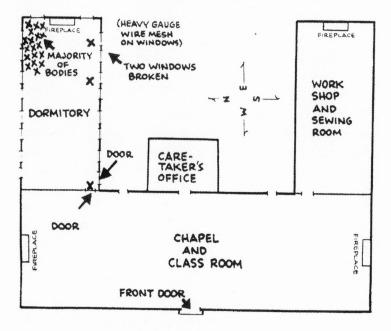

Figure 1. Diagram of Negro Boys Industrial School, March 6, 1959.
Used with permission, *Arkansas Democrat-Gazette*, copyright 1959.

wing on the south end was not used as a dormitory but as a work-shop and contained "a forge, drills and other tools. Toward the front was a sewing room."

The north wing housing the older boys consisted of a large bath-room as they entered the dorm from the chapel, leaving fifty-four feet north to south for use as the sleeping area. The diagram in the *Gazette* article shows the positions of the bodies (marked by the letter "x" for each of the twenty-one bodies.) A *Gazette* reporter explained, "The body of one boy was found in the doorway leading to the chapel. Two more were along the south wall toward the rear and the other 18 were found in a 15-foot space at the two rear win-dows on the north side."

According to the *Arkansas Gazette* account published the morn-ing after the fire, the reaction of some of the "first boys out" was to sprint 150 yards to the residence of Superintendent Lester Gaines. "They brought him back with the keys but there was too much fire to get to the doors. They were never unlocked." The *Gazette* article does not name these boys nor does it provide sources for this information.

More than fifty years later, stories and rumors still abound that Lester Gaines did not spend the night on campus but at his home in Little Rock or even elsewhere. His whereabouts would be only one of the many questions raised about the fire. There were many versions about where people were and what they were doing that night. Fifty-three years later in 2012 on a steamy May morning in Little Rock, a friendly, chance encounter with a well-respected, now retired African American educator underscores the continuing controversy over the fire. "It was a cover-up," he volunteered, after being told about my plan to write a book about the deaths of the boys. It had come to be the standard reaction primarily from members of the African American community in Little Rock.[13] One normally thinks of a cover-up as an intentional act or acts designed to conceal wrongdoing on someone's part; however, as is evident from the newspaper accounts and the story that follows, the word means different things to different people.

◆ ◆ ◆

Chauffeured by the state police, Arkansas governor Orval E. Faubus arrived at the scene about six that morning. The media described him as "angry" and "visibly shaken" by what he encountered. It was not a tableau for the faint of heart. Superintendent Gaines would tell his board of directors of the state-run school that he had not been able to remain at the site: "I finally walked away as I could not stand the odor of bodies being burned."[14]

It was even unnerving for "grizzled" veterans of disaster scenes. Mike McKee, who was then a lieutenant for the Arkansas State Police, recalled it many years later as "one of my most traumatic experiences. . . . It was my job to stand out there and talk to the families of those who died because they came swarming in there from all over."[15] Sheriff's deputies brought from Little Rock twenty prisoners from the Pulaski County Penal Farm to dig through the rubble for remains. By eight in the morning, the twenty-first body was recovered.

It was a scene from the underworld. No human being should have to view the charred remains of children, and it would be in this frame of mind that L. C. Bates, the African American publisher with his wife Daisy of the *Arkansas State Press*, decided not only to destroy the print his photographer had made at the incinerated dormitory, but the negative as well. In an editorial captioned "Is Segregation Worth This?" Bates confided to his readers, "It [the remains of one of the victims]" was "too gruesome to be filed in the morgue."[16] The tragedy was bad enough, but the pain, frustration, and uncertainty of being unable to recognize the body of one's child would gnaw at families for the rest of their lives.

What Orval Faubus and Superintendent Lester Gaines said to each other during the time the governor was on the scene was not recorded, but it could not have been a pleasant conversation as the bodies were removed. A photograph captures the two men standing side by side. The governor is dressed in a familiar dark suit but wearing an overcoat and hat to ward off the March cold and dampness. He appears to be speaking to someone off camera. Superintendent Gaines, appearing exhausted, is wearing a hat, an open-throated shirt, and what appears to be a full-length coat.

Lester Gaines told a reporter that morning that the building had gone up like "matchsticks." The wooden building had only a brick veneer exterior and indeed served as kindling. The structure, built in the 1930s as part of the New Deal federally funded Works Progress Administration program, had burned to the ground. The moment the blaze began would never be precisely established.

If the twenty-one victims ranging in age from thirteen to seventeen had been maniacal arsonists who had burned others to death, perhaps the manner of their deaths could have been considered a kind of macabre poetic justice. To the contrary, Superintendent Gaines told the press that morning that "most of the boys in the dormitory were in for minor offenses, such as hubcap stealing, or because their parents split up and there was no place for them to go." Gaines told UPI reporter Bernie Brown that "one of the boys we lost was sent here when he got picked up soaping windows on Halloween, I understand."[17] Gaines also told a reporter that the "threat of such a tragedy was 'inherent' in the School's budget of $32,000 for salaries. They range from $3,780 for him down to $1,080 a year. He said he had five teachers on the staff."[18]

The agony for the forty-eight who managed to escape continued on into the morning. Reporters wrote that the boys "stood about, some barefoot, and crying, to watch firemen bring out the bodies." Fourteen-year-old George Gray of Little Rock, whose arm had been cut while climbing through a window, "could only manage to stutter his name, age and hometown and say he was cut by a piece of glass." The boys who survived the fire were placed in a classroom that had been converted into a temporary dorm. Arkansas Agricultural, Mechanical & Normal College at Pine Bluff, a predominantly black school funded by the legislature after the Civil War, donated blankets, beds, and mattresses. The "classroom" was at the "little boys'" dorm where the house parents were Dorothy and Winton Mattison. Boys who were cut or burned were taken to the infirmary for treatment. Many were obviously in shock at the horror they were witnessing, but at least they were still alive.

◆ ◆ ◆

Following her early morning routine, North Little Rock resident Ms. Luvenia Long was listening to gospel music on the radio when the program was interrupted for a news bulletin. Church was important to her, but without transportation it was hard to get there with four children. Occasionally, her minister, Horace Johnson, came by and picked up her and the children. Knowing her financial circumstances, he never asked her for money.[19]

Besides her son Lindsey, who was now out at the "school" at Wrightsville, she had three preschool children to raise. A ninth grade dropout herself, Ms. Long had more than enough on her plate in the winter of 1959. As she said, she was no stranger to "hard times." The graveyard already held five of her children, two sets of twins who had died shortly after birth, and Priscilla, who at the age of three had succumbed to whooping cough and pneumonia.

Born in 1926, the year before the last official lynching of a black man across the river in Little Rock, Luvenia had grown up in her mother's house in the Tie Plant area north of the Arkansas River. For more than two decades, there had been work for African American men at the firm of Ayer-Lord Tie Company. Founded in 1907, Ayer-Lord's operation in North Little Rock consisted of the treatment of railroad ties with the preservative creosote. Ayer-Lord "was a major employer ... with more than 300 workers who for the most part lived in the Tie Plant neighborhood near the wood-treatment facility."[20] Too near in fact.

By 1930 the business was owned by the Koppers Company, a major force in the industry. In the early 1950s, Koppers began adding a mixture of chemicals to aid in the process. Chromated copper arsenate and later in the 1960s, Pentachlorophenol (known as PCP) became a part of the mix. If the air smelled bad and the well water had a noxious taste, there wasn't much to do about it. With no means of disposing of the waste, the Tie Plant neighborhood became a toxic dumping ground.

Luvenia's mother Josie Jeffries had grown up in the area. Luvenia didn't know her father. Ms. Jeffries "cleaned up" for white people, and her daughter helped her out by picking and chopping cotton. Luvenia was about ten or eleven when she went to the fields. "We didn't have no water, had to get water from the outside." School was a problem for her. She explained, "I'd laid out so many days I didn't like going to no school," and she dropped out of Scipio A. Jones

High School in North Little Rock. She met her first husband, Charlie Cross, "in a cotton patch." Married at seventeen at the Pulaski County Courthouse in Little Rock, they set up housekeeping in nearby Protho Junction, where conditions were equally dire. Charlie had a part-time job.

Luvenia was twenty-six when she had Lindsey. After two days, she came home with her son from University Hospital across the river in Little Rock. She could have used some help. "Nobody but me and him when I came home." She and Charlie didn't stay together: "He hit me." With her life worse than before her marriage, she remembered, "I came back to Mama" and eventually got a divorce. She continued to do "housework for white people," walking out of the neighborhood of Tie Plant to their homes and working two or three days a week. Her mother worked as a maid as well.

There would be other men in her life and more children. Black men who worked at Koppers were bringing home paychecks, but the money wasn't getting to Luvenia for her children. Men who hadn't assumed their parental obligations had left them with an outhouse, no running water or electricity, and a shotgun house in Tie Plant in which to raise four children: Lindsey, Ellen, Frank, and Greg. Working at a white-owned restaurant on the afternoon and night shift, Ms. Long had to leave the children to look after themselves. When the police drove up to her shack with Lindsey in the backseat in the fall of 1958, Luvenia had no idea what her son had done.[21] The officers took Lindsey into the house. He emerged with an undisclosed sum of money. The details of what happened between the time of his arrest and detention and his commitment to the Negro Boys Industrial School are not clear. His mother had no money for a lawyer but recalls going to an office to see about Lindsey.

Though Luvenia did not remember the path that the law followed in Pulaski County to place her son in an institution, it should not be assumed that Lindsey was hustled off to Wrightsville without some kind of a trial. Howard Lee Nash, also from Pulaski County, remembers his hearing and being ordered to serve five months at

Wrightsville. He had no attorney but did appear before a juvenile judge. That person would have been Mary Burt Nash, whose husband was a partner in one of Little Rock's most prestigious law firms.[22]

Lindsey's name appears on the admission ledger at Wrightsville on January 14, 1959. Less than two months later, he would be one of the victims of the fire. In contrast to many other entries, the ledger is silent as to who brought him out to the Wrightsville facility or the nature of his delinquency. Nor does the ledger recite how long he was to stay. Since 1930 there had been 2,640 admissions into the system. Some of those were repeat admissions.[23] His mother visited him at Wrightsville, but as she said, the Wrightsville institution did not seem like much of a "school" to her.

With the announcement on the radio that some of the boys had been in the fire, Luvenia prevailed upon Buster Sullivan, a neighbor, to drive her to Wrightsville to find out if Lindsey was among the victims. "What they showed me was burnt up bodies all piled up together with a small pile of reddened flesh. There was no way I could identify my boy. No one said anything."[24]

Though some family members said they could and others said they could not identify their children, it would appear to have been guesswork. The remains of what was believed to be Lindsey Cross were taken to Hubble Funeral Home in Little Rock.

Interviewed by her son Frank Lawrence for the documentary he was attempting to make about the fire, his mother remembered,

> There were a couple of meetings between the families, and the ones
> that could recognize or identify their children decided to not have
> them in Heaven [sic] of Rest with the fourteen boys that could not
> be identified, elected to have Dubisson Funeral Home bury them. It
> was decided to take the State up on their offer to bury our sons. . . .
> We were told to leave after Mr. Guy preached the funeral. I wanted to
> stay but there was a policeman who told us to leave that we were not
> allowed to stay. . . . They said we could not look in the caskets either.
> Since the tombstones been removed and the markers for the boys it's

like somebody don't even want to remember they were here. I don't believe they are in the caskets. I believe they are empty. I want one day to have the casket raised and see if I was lied to about the ashes. I just have to know.[25]

On the morning of the funeral, the *Arkansas Gazette* reviewed the arrangements for "the 14 who will be buried in individual caskets but in a mass grave." The article notes that "the mass burial will take place because it has been impossible to identify individually any of the 14 bodies."

As for the other seven victims, Pulaski County coroner Dr. Howard Dishongh reported "that he had identified one of the other boys and that relatives had identified the other six." In fact, there would be some evidence which suggests that families who were said to recognize their sons were not able to do so. Edna Green, the sister of William Lloyd Piggee, stated almost fifty years later, "Up until this day we don't know whether that was my brother or not. They [my parents] just selected a body, but we couldn't recognize him."[26] Hubble Funeral Home, where Lindsey's supposed remains were taken, and Dubisson Undertaking Company were identified in the article as handling the burial arrangements for the fourteen. The question of identification and location of the remains of all twenty-one victims would be raised again almost fifty years later.

At the time of his death on March 5, 1959, Lindsey Cross was his mother's height (five feet two inches) and color (brown-skinned,) but beyond these generalities, after so much time had passed, she understandably had difficulty remembering certain details about her son. Like adolescents everywhere, Lindsey didn't necessarily share his private life with his mother. "He liked basketball," and "he was crazy about his sister," (Ellen, who was almost five), Ms. Long remembered more than fifty years later.[27]

Ellen Wiggins recalled that Lindsey would delight her by throwing her up in the air and catching her. Lindsey went to school and was off playing football or basketball (or so he said), but looking back at his arrest and his death, his mother realized that she didn't know everything about him or his life. If he got into trouble at school, she wasn't told about it. "I never did have problems with him." The boy "was easily influenced."

Not easily influenced at all, according to his cousin Josephine Strickland, who was sixteen at the time of Lindsey's death. When told her Aunt Luvenia had implied Lindsey had followed the pack, Josephine remembered a different personality.[28] She had known Lindsey as a peer. Living "on the next street over" in Tie Plant, Josephine remembered Lindsey, although younger, as already a "leader." Her cousin, she said, loved the "limelight" and was "quick" and "very handsome . . . he knew how to make you laugh. He taught her to play marbles and liked 'cowboy movies,' especially Lash Larue. He loved cars, knew the makes and models." The girls "were crazy about him." Lindsey liked "clothes" and not long after the robbery of Puckett's store in Tie Plant, she saw him wearing a new "red cap."[29] She says she wondered then if he might have been involved in the robbery. Buddy Green, who was also arrested, had "lived across the street from my grandmother." According to Josephine, it was a neighbor, Carrie Wright, who may have told the white owner that it was Lindsey who had stolen the money.

Whether Lindsey was the Pied Piper or a youth with too much time on his hands after school, according to his "delayed" birth certificate he was only thirteen years old, not fifteen, as he would be listed in the paper.[30] But even if Lindsey had been a "mama's boy" and had wanted to confide in her, his mother would have been hard-pressed to make the time.

◆ ◆ ◆

Though the belief that children and adolescents would benefit from a separate criminal jurisprudence had begun to take hold at the turn of the twentieth century throughout the United States, initially the motivation for reform school legislation in Arkansas was, in the words of juvenile law professor Paula Casey, "perhaps . . . not so much the rehabilitation and reform of juveniles as it was to get the convicted juveniles off the streets and confine them." After all, Jeff Davis, the sitting governor, routinely pardoned juveniles because, as he said, "it would be outrageous to confine them in an ordinary penitentiary with the worst element of criminals in our state."[31] Whatever the motive, almost any legislation would have been better than nothing. In 1892, for example, approximately 20 percent of the inmates in the Arkansas State Penitentiary were not yet twenty-one. In that year, a nine-year-old was convicted and served time with adults. Black and white Arkansas sharecroppers who were desperate to feed their families after having been routinely cheated by their landlords were understandably sometimes not adverse to larceny. Historian John Graves quotes John W. Williams, a black state senator from Phillips County in 1885, who argued against a bill making the theft of an item worth more than two dollars a crime punishable by one to five years in prison. The bill also required that anything under that amount was a misdemeanor with a maximum sentence of a year and a three hundred dollar fine. Williams predicted that if the bill passed, and it did, "poor whites and blacks will be driven to the pen." Theft landed blacks disproportionately in the penitentiary, and it was for stealing "petty sums" according to the *Arkansas Gazette*, that most convicts (414 out of 552 in 1877–1878) were serving time. Though constituting just under a fourth of the state's population, blacks sometimes outnumbered whites in the penitentiary by as much as two to one.[32]

What came out of the 1905 legislative session could only be called reform under the most generous of definitions. In the words of an early Arkansas historian, "Writ large over this measure is the legislative conception that the school was to be a place of punishment for bad children."[33]

Educating children caught up in the adult criminal process was not a priority of the legislators who mandated that the maximum time in any one year at Arkansas's "reform school" that could be spent on "literary studies" was three months. On the other hand, section 7 of Act 199 required that "everything practicable shall be done to develop them morally, intellectually and industriously, and to teach them some useful trade or avocation." In fact, learning to read, add, and subtract and keeping careful accounts of expenses and credit might have been a useful skill for someone who was determined to try to keep himself, his parents, and brothers and sisters from being cheated.

Proposed by Governor Jeff Davis, the "reform" act provided in Section 10 that "white and negro inmates . . . shall, at all times on all occasions, be kept separate and apart from each other, and the female inmates shall be kept to themselves." If education was not a priority for these children, especially black children, it was not an accident. In 1904 Jeff Davis had campaigned for reelection on the slogan, "Every time you educate a 'nigger' you spoil a good field hand." By 1905 his message to the Arkansas legislature included an unrestrained diatribe against blacks, in which he said, in part,

> We have come, in my judgment, to the parting of the ways with the negro. We have tried to be his friend, we have tried to educate him, we have tried to teach him Christian morality . . . but let one of the . . . Republicans get a crowd of "niggers" in a back alley, or in a "nigger" church and make an inflammatory speech to them, and the good we have tried to do for years will be wiped away in a moment; . . . any effort upon the part of Arkansas or the Southland to further divide her blessings with this degenerate and improvident race is futile. A Negro is not susceptible of higher education, he is not susceptible of higher moral culture.
>
> A negro is a servant made so by God Almighty, bred and born as such, and no matter with what tender solicitude we attempt to raise him up from his position, he is but a servant still. Attempted education proves harmful rather than beneficial. . . . From this day forward let the negroes in Arkansas educate themselves. . . . The South for nearly half a century has done her best to try to make something out of the negro, and we have totally failed.[34]

What Davis was proposing was passage of a bill to fund segregated public education by the tax revenues collected from each race. The intention was "white taxes for white schools only," a legislative measure Raymond Arsenault, the governor's most prominent biographer, notes, had it passed, "would virtually destroy the state's black educational system." As appealing as the proposal was to some representatives from "the Black Belt counties of south Arkansas," the bill was decisively defeated by "legislators [who] were unwilling to support a measure that promised to exacerbate an already troublesome labor shortage."[35]

Though Arsenault acknowledges that "Davis was something of an extremist on the segregated school tax issue" as well as a "committed white supremacist and a gifted Negrophobic propagandist," he argues persuasively that Davis never forgot he was a politician. Citing examples, Arsenault writes that Davis "tailored his actions to political realities, not to racial theories. . . . He was, in the fullest sense of the term, a racial 'demagogue,' an on-again-off-again bigot who knew when to use the racial issue and when not to."[36]

Less than half a century later, another popular Arkansas governor would see some similarities between himself and Jeff Davis. But not for one moment did Orval Eugene Faubus see himself as a racial bigot or demagogue who presided over a state intent on keeping black people down. Nor did a significant number of his constituents, whether white or black, view the governor, then on his third term, as someone hostile to the interests of the minority population. Yet beginning with the Central High desegregation crisis, he had become a lightning rod for criticism by persons outside the state.

In its entirety, a hand-printed letter from Mrs. Marion Ingham in New Brunswick, New Jersey, on the night of the fire is scathing:

> Dear Governor, I have just read the story in to-night's paper about the
> fire in Little Rock. I could vomit every time I think of what your state
> has done in public relations as far as a world view is concerned, of
> the United States. Do you realize how far the small state of Arkansas

has put us <u>back</u>?–and I as a citizen of this great nation hold <u>you</u> responsible.[37]

Luville Milton from San Mateo, California, wrote on March 8,

My dear Governor Faubus, Each time I see in the newspaper a by-line 'Little Rock, Arkansas,' I shudder because I know it means yet another atrocity against the Negroes. . . . With all my heart and soul, with the full strength of my being, I utterly condemn the treatment of Negroes by the government and people of the state of Arkansas.[38]

Nineteen months earlier, the photograph of Elizabeth Eckford being hounded and cursed by whites on the grounds of Central High School in the capital city of Little Rock had horrified people around the world. Occurring at a crucial time in the nation's Cold War against the Soviet Union in 1957, the photographs, images, and stories and coming out of Little Rock had been a public relations disaster for the nation that billed itself as the world's greatest democracy, a defender of freedom and a beacon of light for oppressed people throughout the planet. All fifteen-year-old Elizabeth Eckford and eight other black classmates had been trying to do was assert their constitutional, court-ordered right to get an education at Central High School. What kind of Americans curse and bully defenseless children in front of the rest of the world? What kind of Americans allow their government to decline to prosecute individuals who physically assault reporters and photographers with the entire planet watching?

United Press International (UPI) wire service immediately distributed the story about the incineration of twenty-one boys locked in from the outside in a wooden firetrap of a dormitory with rotten floors and frayed wiring in a no longer quite so obscure part of the South. Not one to give ammunition to his detractors, Governor Orval E. Faubus didn't see fit to make these letters available for public scrutiny. They were ignored for almost fifty years, as was the fire itself after initial coverage by the media. But it would not have mattered. White Arkansans didn't see themselves the same way as did these angry and anguished uninvited correspondents. One of the two in-state letters the governor received directly related to the fire at this time was wholly sympathetic to him. Former Hot Springs radio broadcaster Walter M. Ebel wrote on March 6 in part, "I believe I know how truly you regret this [the fire and the deaths of the boys]." He suggested that Faubus call a "joint session" of the legislature and ask for funds for a "new and modern school."[39]

For the most part, Arkansans didn't blame Governor Faubus for the deaths of the boys; nor did the fact that their deaths had occurred in a racially segregated institution suggest to most Arkansans that this tragedy might be a moral issue that anything to do with white supremacy. Yet Orval Faubus had not gotten where he was by leaving anything to chance. Almost always ahead of his critics, he called a press conference almost as soon as he returned from the scene of the fire. There was damage control to be done as only he could do it.[40]

CHAPTER TWO

The Second Most Powerful Governor

[Faubus] amassed enormous political power in his state, perhaps
more than any other American governor except that which Huey P.
Long acquired in neighboring Louisiana a generation earlier.
He knew the value of a good enemy. He sometimes saw himself as a
modern, somewhat subtler version of Jeff Davis, the famous turn-of-
the-century governor who profited by using the capital as a foil.
—**Roy Reed**, *Faubus: The Life and Times of an American Prodigal*

By mid-morning, Orval Eugene Faubus was in his office at the Capitol in Little Rock working on a statement for the press conference
he would be holding later about the fire. As unnerved as he was by
the grotesqueness of what he had just witnessed, he knew, given the
opportunity, his enemies might try to dump the ashes of twenty-one
Negro boys at the doorstep of the Governor's Mansion if he didn't
head them off.

The governor understood he had to protect himself from criticism for not having previously asked the legislature for money
to replace the dormitory that had just burned. As he had already
alluded to earlier that morning, in January 1958 the state police
had driven him from Little Rock on a Saturday to inspect both
the institution at Wrightsville and the white girls' school outside of
Pine Bluff. What he found at Wrightsville was worse than he had
expected. He told the press that day, "They really need help. They are
using some old wood stoves which should be replaced; the floors
have been scrubbed until they are rotten in the dormitories, kitchen

and dining room. The store room is the worst building I have seen anywhere. The school is set up for an operation of 30 years ago, and it is time to improve it."[1]

But instead of including an appropriation for the construction of new dormitories at Wrightsville in the more than four years he had been in office, he had done no more than instruct Mack Sturgis, his good friend whom he had appointed state purchasing agent, to contact the state penitentiary board and persuade it to take some of the convicts to Wrightsville on a work detail to pull down some of the dilapidated buildings (an old cotton gin and warehouse) at the school and do some general clean up. Mack had responded that the penitentiary board had sent a "committee" to survey what needed to be done. He wrote that they "found, of course, the institution in a deplorable and disgusting condition," but as a favor to the governor, the "committee" had agreed to send "twelve of their best men" to put in "three days work."

As "pay," the Penitentiary Board would take the contents as "salvage." Mack had talked to Alfred Smith, chairman of the NBIS Board who thought the contents should be put up for bids, but Mack explained to the governor it was just "junk" and couldn't be sold.[2] The Negro Boys Industrial School at Wrightsville had never been a priority for him as governor, and he had actually reduced the appropriation for the school during his first term in office from the previous biennium by $7,100.[3] After appointing a board as he was required by law to do, he had paid little attention to the institution until his visit, not even appointing replacements for two board members whose terms had expired months earlier before the fire.

It wasn't that he didn't have time, since he often worked eighteen hours a day and personally wrote detailed responses to some of the many letters he received, not just from Arkansans but American citizens from all over the country. He made time for everything. At the end of December 1958, the influential George Gallup Poll had surveyed Americans and asked the following: "What man that you have heard or read about, living today in any part of the world, do you admire the most?" Confounding his enemies, he had made the list, placing tenth.

Ahead of him were such heroes of the American imagination as Winston Churchill, Dr. Albert Schweitzer, Douglas MacArthur, Billy Graham, Harry Truman, and Eisenhower's vice president Richard Nixon. Faubus's nemesis, President Dwight D. Eisenhower, had placed first. But Orval Faubus had been the only governor or member of Congress in 1958 to make the list.

As a courtesy, the Gallup Poll had given those on the list advance notice before the results was released to the public, and he had made most of the opportunity by contacting the *Arkansas Democrat*, which sent a photographer to the mansion. He picked his words carefully in responding to the honor, saying modestly, "The selection really surprises me because I didn't believe we had that much support.... It shows a great number of people agree with what I've stood for, so far as the principles of government are concerned."[4]

Sounding like a candidate (though he realized he was the longest of long shots for national office) and with two two-year terms under his belt as governor, he had warned against "centralized government," saying, "I would like to see a greater understanding of the virtues of democracy, with the proper understanding of local and state responsibility as solutions to today's problems. Therein, I firmly believe, lies the preservation of our great liberties and American way of life."[5]

Former *New York Times* reporter and subsequent college professor Roy Reed wrote an exhaustively researched biography, *Faubus: The Life and Times of an American Prodigal* (1999), which preserves for history one of the most complicated figures in American politics.[6] Morbidly shy as a boy, Orval Faubus would later remember that as a schoolteacher meeting his first class of raw-boned hill country kids—his own people—he ran a fever for weeks but had no other symptoms of illness. If his monumental insecurity approached a pathological condition among his own kind, one could appreciate what he felt in 1954 as governor among the sophisticated movers and shakers who controlled Little Rock from the posh environs of the Little Rock Country Club (LRCC) in the Heights.

In the words of Reed, Faubus's wife Alta was a "good country woman" but one who would hardly qualify as a candidate for membership in the LRCC. Not only was she miserable in Little Rock, but their son, Ferrell, was bullied at Central High School and would persuade his father to let him finish at Huntsville. Ferrell was lucky. Faubus told Alta that if she tried to leave him, he would send the state police to bring her back.

All his life he had compensated for his humble background and his natural shyness by adopting a reserved formality in his dealings with the public. A photograph of him in a dark suit asking for a voter's support in a barbershop captured his gravity and seriousness while involved in an endeavor more noted for its affected affability and forced friendliness. In face-to-face encounters he treated people, including black Arkansans, with courtesy and dignity. It was crucial to his own sense of self-worth not to be dismissed as a yokel.[7] This facet of his character was, of course, particularly important to African Americans and much appreciated even by some of his enemies. After a meeting with the governor in 1957 about legislation that would affect the National Association for the Advancement of Colored People (NAACP), Daisy Bates found him without the usual condescension she often experienced in dealing with whites. "Very gracious," she wrote about him.[8]

Eighteen months before the Wrightsville fire during the arguably most serious constitutional crisis the country had then faced in the twentieth century, Faubus and the president of the United States had squared off (at least in the governor's view) over "the proper understanding of local and state responsibility." In September 1957, in a broadcast on statewide television, and without pointing a finger or raising his voice, he calmly explained to the people of Arkansas that he had ordered the National Guard to surround Central High School. He justified his decision by saying that he had received reports that there would be violence if Negroes were admitted to Central.

But he had also devoted almost three pages of his ten-page speech to detailing the progress Negroes were making in Arkansas. Negroes had been attending the University of Arkansas for some time and were now enrolled in all the other state-supported colleges. They were serving "on both the Republican and Democratic state central committees." They had benefited from his successful efforts to raise the salaries of black teachers. Likewise, during his tenure they had received significant welfare and pension increases along with whites. They had jobs in state government. They "had been integrated into the public school systems of the state where it was acceptable to the majority and could be peaceably accomplished."[9]

It seemed the whole world had seen the picture of Elizabeth Eckford at Central High being cursed by whites on September 3, 1957, when she tried to enter the school. That photograph and others of reporters being beaten had triggered the start of an avalanche of hate mail against him and the state. The NAACP could not have asked for a better fund-raising letter.

Before he found his footing on the September 14, he had allowed Brooks Hays, Arkansas's US Representative from Little Rock, talk him into flying up to Newport, Rhode Island, to meet President Eisenhower personally to resolve the crisis. Orval, an intelligence officer in World War II, had agreed, thinking he could persuade the old general to at least let him buy some time. Let the courts continue to sort it out. True, a federal judge had ordered the Little Rock School Board to go forward with integration of Central, but so what? It had taken more than a century to get this far, so what were a few more months? Lawyers asked for delays of proceedings all the time. As it turned out, Attorney General Herbert Brownell was the fly in the ointment, advising the president against compromise. The meeting with Ike on September 14 at Newport, Rhode Island, proved to be a disaster. Eisenhower came away from their private visit with the understanding that Faubus had agreed to withdraw the troops and allow the Negro children to enter. However, the next day he exercised the prerogative of changing his mind, feebly telling the media, "Just because I said it doesn't make it so."[10]

He took a lot of flak for that remark, but by August 1957 he felt he was in an impossible position. From an area of the state that had almost no Negroes, he hadn't come to Little Rock to hold back blacks but to lift out of poverty his own people—the hard-scrabble farmers from the hill country. He had worked for and with Sid McMath, whose reform efforts as a two-term governor had crashed and burned over a scandal in the Arkansas Highway Department.

As governor, Faubus at first had mostly tried to duck the issue of school integration, saying that it was a local issue. If school boards voted to integrate, he would not interfere. The US Supreme Court had ruled in *Brown v. Board of Education* (1954) that public schools must allow black children to go to school with whites. According to Roy Reed, on one occasion, Faubus had told friends that he would have voted with the 9 to 0 majority had he been on the Court. And he stayed out of the conflict that developed at Hoxie in 1955 in northeast Arkansas after the school board had voted to bring a handful of black children into its all-white system. Earlier in that year, the Supreme Court had ruled that there might be reasons why a school district could ask for a delay, but otherwise the Court expected districts to integrate with "all deliberate speed."

Race, however, was an issue that was not going to leave him or any southern politician alone, and if he wasn't going to weigh in decisively on the issue of school integration, others would. In 1956 almost every member of Congress from the Old Confederacy, including Arkansas's two senators and six representatives, signed the so-called Southern Manifesto, pledging to do everything short of violence to overturn the *Brown* decision. With the southern winds of "massive resistance" now reaching hurricane force, it became progressively harder to hunker down and hope the windbags in Congress blew themselves out. As someone who despite the occasional heartburn now more easily digested the irresistible fruits of power, Orval didn't see he had a choice if he wanted to remain in the governor's chair.

Among gubernatorial candidates within Arkansas, nobody rang the race bell louder than Jim Johnson, a handsome spellbinder of a speaker from Crossett down in the southern part of the state. Jim could heat up a racial fire hotter and quicker than anyone around with outrageous stories of race mixing and Communist influence. From politicians like Jim who enjoyed his political meat bloody as often as not, Faubus had learned that if you wanted to win, you had to play hardball whatever the issue was. He had beaten Jim in 1956, but he hadn't wanted to face him again. At least Jim wasn't a hypocrite like Francis Cherry, whom he had beaten in 1954.

In the mind of Orval Faubus, nobody could have been more ineffectual than his predecessor, Francis Cherry, who totally wasted his time trying to reform the way state government did its business. His obsession with creating higher ethical standards for state government accomplished little except to alienate important business interests whose support was crucial for programs to lift the state out of the poverty in which it had been mired since the Civil War. Cherry had thought all a governor needed to do was to stand up and make a speech and that the legislature would fall all over itself doing whatever he wanted. Cherry hadn't known what he wanted, or how to get it. And even if he had known, Francis acted like he was too good to get his hands dirty. Previously he had been a family-law judge, which had suited him perfectly. His becoming governor was a textbook example of a man rising to the level of his incompetence. As a judge, he could hide behind his robe and pontificate all he wanted, then sign an order telling people what to do and call the next case. Faubus's view was that men like Cherry were a dime a dozen, especially in Little Rock. Just like the rest of the silk-stocking crowd in the Heights, Cherry had proved to be the rankest of hypocrites—acting as if he were Mr. Ethics during his one term as governor but acting just like everyone else when he found himself running behind Faubus during the runoff campaign for reelection.

Desperate to kill Faubus's momentum, Cherry, the challenger had learned, was going to question his patriotism by bringing up the fact that for a few weeks in the 1930s he had attended Commonwealth College in Mena, which had preached socialism. This tactic showed how low the so-called upper class could stoop.

Faubus heard later that Francis had thrown up right on the front porch of the governor's mansion before going on television to try to smear him. Showed you how gutless the man was. If you were going to play hardball, you needed the stomach for it. Whatever else they could say about him, nobody could question Faubus's patriotism or his courage. He had nearly been killed in the Battle of the Bulge. True, his campaign literature made him seem as if he had served longer than he had, but in his mind that was just politics.

Faubus believed he did the only thing he could do and win—lying about how long and under what circumstances he had attended Commonwealth, but thanks to some help from the same uppercrust crowd that Cherry ran with, he had made the charge backfire on Cherry. Harry Ashmore, the super smart South Carolinian who had been recruited to come to Little Rock and become the editor of the *Arkansas Gazette*, had written Faubus a masterful speech that made voters angry over Cherry's tactics. With this help, he squeaked in by just a little over six thousand votes and never looked back.

For almost two terms, Ashmore and the *Gazette* backed him as he battled the legislature for increased compensation for teachers, raises in pensions for old people, and increases in welfare for the poor. It turned out that he was the liberal, and the fat cats in the Heights the conservatives. They didn't care about the working stiffs in Little Rock, and they didn't like him once they found out they couldn't control or outsmart him.

Government must help the needy, especially those from his own region of the state, Faubus believed. Especially during the Great Depression during the 1930s, Arkansas was desperately poor. While the Delta sharecroppers, both black and white, received most of the country's attention, his people, the dirt-poor farmers in the Ozarks, suffered grievously as well. He had left the state during the Depression to pick fruit more than once to survive. His deepest instinct was for the underdog, albeit hill-country style and white in color.

Unlike his father, however, he wasn't resigned to always be on the losing side. An out-and-out socialist who ended up more of a populist, it was his father Sam who had persuaded him to try Commonwealth College near the Oklahoma border, and to please him Orval had. He had lasted three months, had even been elected president of the student body, but the place was crawling with radicals, later even Communists. If he had known what Commonwealth was like, he wouldn't have gotten within a country mile of the place. He knew his lies and dissembling about Commonwealth had made the difference in the election, but under the circumstances, they were easy to justify. Politics, he had quickly learned, was a "grand game."[11]

Faubus also learned rapidly that to do good for people, sometimes you had to bend the rules, because other people didn't play by the rules. Three years later Ashmore and his ilk, the silk-stocking Little Rock Heights crowd, had expected him to be a sacrificial lamb and do the federal government's job of integrating the schools and take the political hit from the rabid segregationists who were howling for him to stop integration in Little Rock.

Everyone squeezed him as hard as they could. On one end were the Citizens Councils, Jim Johnson, and Red-baiters who were popping up every five minutes in Little Rock. On the other were people like Ashmore and the *Gazette* crowd, Little Rock school superintendent Virgil Blossom, and even Winthrop Rockefeller, his Republican millionaire industry recruiter, telling him to take a blowtorch to the face and let the black kids in Central. He wouldn't have gotten five votes if he hadn't taken a stand.

For awhile things had gone from bad to worse. With Eisenhower turning him down, the NAACP was back in court persuading Ronald Davies, the Yankee out-of-state visiting federal judge who now exercised jurisdiction over the Little Rock integration case, to issue an order prohibiting him from using the National Guard to stop integration at Central. As he had said he would do all along, he obeyed the judge's ruling and ordered the National Guard to stand down.

Faubus was out of the state attending the Southern Governors' Conference when the NAACP tried again on September 23 to force the nine students into Central. Though historian Elizabeth Jacoway has documented that Faubus somehow may not have known that Daisy Bates had decided that the 23rd would be the day the Little Rock Nine would make another attempt to enter Central, the governor would have known the possibility of the violence that would ensue. Faubus's failure to return to Little Rock immediately was inexcusable.[12] He had openly predicted violence yet failed to discourage the mob outside Central, which was out in full force. The nine black children had to be sneaked out of the school that afternoon. The next day, Eisenhower ordered troopers from the 158th Airborne Division in Ft. Campbell, Kentucky, to Little Rock to make sure the Nine got into Central and stayed.

The South had been invaded by federal troops once again, and as Governor Faubus made sure the rest of the country realized what the consequences were and what could be done about it. The repercussions were immediate as well as long term. An army of occupation settled in with fixed bayonets. Soldiers literally patrolled the halls of Central High. Turmoil prevailed during the entire school year. As expected by many observers, however, the US Supreme Court refused in September 1958 to affirm Arkansas federal district judge Harry Lemley's decision to grant a two-and-a-half-year delay in desegregating Central. Not to be outsmarted, the governor already had in place a plan that quickly resulted in the closing of the Little Rock public high schools.[13]

Working with his wealthy personal physician and close friend T. J. Raney, in October 1958 he helped engineer the opening of a private high school in Little Rock.[14] Supported in part by tax dollars, the private school was being challenged in the courts by the

NAACP, but who knew what the federal judiciary would do? After all, the Supreme Court had backed off its original 1954 decision to require immediate integration in the public schools by issuing another opinion a year later. In what was called *Brown II*, the Court had held that there could be good reasons for a school district to ask for a delay.

In January 1959 the governor attended a reception at the newly opened Raney High School, a private school in Little Rock. There he was mobbed by well-wishers. Nicknamed (of course!) the Rebels, the Raney High School band had played "Dixie," just as it had at his inauguration.

Now at the tail end of the ongoing legislative session, the governor had gotten most of what he wanted in the way of legislation dealing with the racial issue. At the moment, he was fighting tooth and nail for a bill that would allow him to appoint three new members to the Little Rock School Board and was applying all the pressure he could. His allies and enemies on the Little Rock School Board were split three to three, but if he could get this bill through the session, his supporters could carry out their purge of teachers and administrators thought to be sympathetic to integration.

But now he had to deal with the fire.

◆ ◆ ◆

At his 10 a.m. press conference, the governor of Arkansas announced a plan to conduct his own inquiry "to find the guilty in the tragedy as well as to absolve the innocent."[15] But in fact, moments earlier he had put the finishing touches on his version of the fire for the press before any investigation could begin. Reporters were like children, he believed: if you didn't hold their hands and lead them in the right direction, they could get you into trouble in a heartbeat.

In essence, his written statement indicted Lester Gaines: "A Negro boy was on duty in the recreation room.... The Negro superintendent had not entrusted him with keys to the locked doors. He had to break out of the main building to run for help. By this time it was too late for any of the boys to escape through the door. Those who escaped got out through the broken windows."[16]

Faubus's written comments also called attention to the fact that "all the personnel of the school are Negroes, and the board is composed of three Negroes and two white men." But going down this road would quickly turn out to be a minefield, and he would have to back off. As mentioned previously, not only did state law require the appointment of two "Negroes" on the five-person Wrightsville board, but Faubus realized that the press would soon be alerted to the fact that the board he had appointed seemed to be barely functioning. In fact, one of the black members was not considered a member any longer. His appointee, I. S. McClinton, an influential black political figure and activist in Pulaski County and sometime enemy of L. C. and Daisy Bates, acknowledged to the media that his term had expired. Though he was eligible to attend meetings until his replacement took his seat, he had not received notice of the meetings since November 1958. It seemed that this state board was not providing much oversight. A white board member, Claude Marsh of Searcy, had resigned in October, and the governor had not filled his position either. These vacancies looked bad, but all he could do was have Rolla issue a statement "that the fact that Marsh and McClinton weren't reappointed had nothing to do with last week's fire."[17]

He appeared to be on more solid ground with his statement on March 5 that "there's absolutely no reason for this to happen the way it did except because of negligence on the part of someone."[18] In his written statement, he said that "plans already 'were under consideration by this legislature to provide funds to make improvements to the buildings at the school," but in his state of the state message to the legislature at his inauguration in January 1959, there was no mention of his plan to improve the institution.[19] He pointed out that "a new one-story fire-resistant school" had just been completed less than a year earlier at the Fargo Training School for Negro Girls near Brinkley, but this had nothing to do with the fire and by way of contrast highlighted the deficiencies at Wrightsville.[20]

To buttress the contention that he had no responsibility for the fire, Faubus, in his prepared statement, gave the specifics of his prior visit to the school, noting that he "had 'inspected closely' the School a year ago with Superintendent L. R. Gaines and that he had given 'especial attention' to the safety features, fire extinguishers, means of ingress and egress. He said he had believed the safety precautions were adequate."

A reporter asked if a fire like this could happen at other state institutions. "No," he responded, "this was perhaps the worst facility of them all, and it would not have happened here if adequate precautions had been taken."[21]

No reporters followed up on what could have been a damaging admission by asking him why he had waited four years to do something about the school. With this statement, he might have realized his response could be interpreted by his detractors as having accepted some responsibility for the condition of the dormitory. He had acknowledged in response to another question that a number of state-owned buildings, "including the old buildings at the Little Rock unit of the State Hospital," were "in the fire-trap" class. "I know it and ever since I have been down here, I have been trying to do something about them."

No one asked why, if he was so concerned about fire hazards, he had not interrogated his superintendent about the wiring in the boys' dormitory. Asked why the doors were locked, he had responded, "The school has been plagued by runaways."[22] Again, no one challenged this assertion. Nor did anyone attempt to compare the number of runaways at Wrightsville with the number of runaways at the white boys' school in Pine Bluff.

The media checked on the white boys' school in Pine Bluff and reported the next day that the boys were not locked in at night and that two house parents were always on duty.[23] Halfway into the lead article in the *Gazette* on March 6, the words "Cause Not Known" were printed in boldface. Reporter Joe Wirges wrote that the state police's deputy state fire marshal, W. C. Struebing (who had gotten to Wrightsville before the first body had been removed), "and other firemen were fairly certain that the blaze began in the attic and probably in the front of the building over or near the caretaker's room." How the fire started was seen as more problematic. "Perhaps in the wiring, firemen said, or maybe from lightning."

Asked at his press conference if he thought a white person had set the fire "because of the integration situation," Faubus replied, "I think that can be ruled out completely. . . . I can't conceive of any connection between the fire and the racial situation. Of course with the type of boys you have at an institution like that, it's not unusual for inmates to set fires to escape. . . . Whether this was done I don't know."[24]

Since there was no fence around the institution and boys could and did escape during the day or night before they were locked in at 10 p.m., the suggestion that a boy would deliberately set a fire inside the dormitory at night as part of an attempt to flee made little sense. Rather, it was a typical Faubus response to avoid the suggestion that his own actions, however indirectly, might have led to the fire.

His cursory dismissal of the chance that the incident was connected with the ongoing school integration crisis did not rule the possibility out, for a good portion of the state's history of white supremacy was a chronicle of intimidation by fire. Sometimes intended as a warning, sometimes something more, destruction of black schools by whites was a regular occurrence in Arkansas history.

Historian Story Matkin-Rawn has documented the destruction of one Arkansas black school after another, beginning in the World War I era. To make sure African Americans got the point, "the boys' dormitory and chapel of the Walter Institute in Warren, a well-respected private black academy owned by the A.M.E. church, was burned twice." Matkin-Rawn concludes that "the builders of [the] Arkansas black public school system had to proceed with caution.

When local whites felt threatened by black institution building, schools were often the first targets of sabotage."[25]

Arkansan Lee Wilson, owner of the fabled fifty-thousand-acre Delta Empire in Mississippi County, learned in 1924 that it made no difference whether the benefactor of the school was black or white, private or public. Wilson had contributed $52,500 of his own money to build a "state-of-the-art" industrial school for African Americans. His biographer, the historian Jeannie Whayne, writes, "The burning of the black school . . . revealed the resentment some whites continued to feel for blacks and exposed, once again, the vulnerability of African Americans in a racially charged environment."[26]

No one, especially not Orval Faubus, could have denied on the day of the fire that the environment in Arkansas was "racially charged." In the previous two years, whites had regularly lit fiery crosses and tossed firebombs on the property of black civil rights leaders L. C. and Daisy Bates in Little Rock. Typically, no one was arrested for the harassment and attempted murder of black civil rights leaders, and it would be only when Labor Day bombs later in the year exploded at the office of the Little Rock School District office and at the business of the city's new mayor that an arrest was made and a conviction was obtained. Interestingly, it was Orval Faubus who would arrange for the release of E. A. Lauderdale, the convicted bomber. A Capital Citizens' Council member, Lauderdale had served just six months of a three-year sentence. Perhaps as an afterthought, the governor saw to it that the fine of $500 was returned to Lauderdale.[27]

After reading the afternoon *Arkansas Democrat* the morning of the fire, the governor must surely have asked himself why he hadn't removed Gaines the moment he, Faubus, had taken office and installed his own superintendent. With Lester Gaines shooting off his mouth to the press about how innocent these boys were and how little money his staff received, the fire could come back on him as governor. That's what he should have done. His own man would have kept his mouth shut without having to be told. It was a needless and totally uncharacteristic mistake. A governor appoints people who understand their first job and sometimes their only job is to remember whose hand is feeding them.

Within twenty-four hours, Faubus would appoint the Wrightsville board, the state police, and the state fire marshal—all under his control—to conduct an immediate investigation of the fire. He also began the process of requesting an appropriation from the legislature to rebuild the burned-out dorm and authorize the payment from the Governor's Emergency Fund for the funerals of the fourteen boys whose remains would be buried in the all-black Haven of Rest Cemetery.

Orval Faubus now ran closer to the ground, and in the winter of 1959 nothing moved faster than the mind of the governor when he sensed the possibility that his enemies would try to force him to take responsibility for something that could do him political harm. He would occasionally appear trapped by his critics, but Houdini-like, he would escape, leaving friend and foe alike to wonder where and how the governor had vanished. He and his enemies both used a homely metaphor to describe the process: the governor had disappeared into one of his "holes," a metaphor that suggests the craftiness and clever nature of a fox who outwits his enemies. Before long, L. C. Bates, one of his most persistent critics, would accuse him of using race to try to disappear into one of his "holes" to avoid responsibility for the fire.

CHAPTER THREE

Explaining the Fire

I was so shook up I didn't know what I was saying. I should have
had myself locked up where you newspapermen couldn't get to me.
—**Lester Gaines**, *Arkansas Gazette*, March 6, 1959

When the city edition of the March 5, 1959, afternoon *Arkansas Democrat* hit the streets just hours after the fire was extinguished, Lester "Buddy" Gaines knew without a doubt he was in the crosshairs of the governor. The ashes of the destroyed dormitory weren't even cold but he was being blamed for twenty-one of the worst deaths imaginable. It seemed every other word out of the governor's mouth was aimed at him. Earlier that day he had been his own worst enemy. On the front page of the *Arkansas Democrat* that afternoon was the paragraph that would dog him the rest of his life: "There was no adult attendant in the building last night. The regular attendant is ill and in a hospital, and School Supt. L. R. Gaines said he 'didn't think it was necessary to assign another adult to sleep in the dormitory at night.' He said, 'We had a night sergeant there . . . and an adult checked to see that the boys got in bed at night and up in the morning.'"[1] But in telling a reporter he didn't think it was "necessary" to have an adult present all night at the dormitory with the older boys, Buddy Gaines obviously did not understand at the moment he made this remark how damning it appeared. Putting this remark in context with his other statements to reporters that morning about the conditions at the school, the superintendent would not have necessarily foreseen that anything he said

38

earlier in the day could be taken as an admission of his negligence or even a mild criticism of the governor. His intended audience appears to have been the Arkansas legislature, or more specifically the members of the Legislative Council. Routinely, superintendents and agency heads were required to appear before the council and explain their proposed budgets.

An afternoon editorial about the fire from a stalwart ally of the governor got at the points Gaines had been making that morning. By characterizing the situation at the school as a result of a "long history of neglect" and concluding that the deaths of the boys were on the "conscience of Arkansas," the opinion piece titled "Tragedy at Wrightsville" suggested that responsibility for the fire went far beyond the actions of any individual. The unsigned editorial spoke knowledgeably about the conditions at the school, stating that "almost all the physical plant was allowed to deteriorate, and when that problem was brought up now and then opinion was divided on what should be done. Aside from the financial question, there was a feeling the school should be relocated."

The author of the editorial claimed dangers to the public were systemic in another institution as well. "Out at the State Hospital several thousand sick people are confined to buildings that are fire traps. Again hospital authorities are pleading for new construction, for they have lived in constant dread of a fire breaking out."[2] Though few Arkansans would have likely been aware of it, the writer of the editorial was surely K. August Engel, the publisher of the *Arkansas Democrat*. A supporter of the governor's racial policies, Engel only rarely wrote editorials.

A native of Luckenbach, Texas, and the grandson of a Lutheran minister, Engel was deeply conservative, both in his personal habits and views and in the way he ran his paper. "Early to bed, early to rise," he lived alone in an apartment at the Albert Pike Hotel in downtown Little Rock and walked to work each morning to the *Democrat*. His only apparent indulgence was that he played golf on Thursday and Sunday at the Little Rock Country Club. He was the boss. Every week he paid his employees in cash. But he was also a citizen member of the board that oversaw state agencies that dealt with social welfare issues, and it was in this capacity that he became well-informed about the problems at Wrightsville and other institutions operated by the state.[3]

His editorial in no way suggested that the governor shared responsibility for the deaths at Wrightsville, pointing out that the year before, Faubus had made a surprise visit to the school and had talked to reporters about its "great needs there." In fact, the editorial could be read as a defense of him. After all, in 1957 the governor had secured "an appropriation for new facilities" at the Negro Girls Training School. He had called the buildings at that school "a disgrace to the state." Though the difficulties at all black institutions run by the state, including Wrightsville, were rooted in much deeper causes, the problem, according to publisher Engel, was that "in the competition of state agencies for funds, the Negro boys' school never fared well."[4]

For Buddy Gaines, normally the most gregarious of men, the day was a continuing nightmare as firemen and police explained to hysterical mothers that the child they had given birth to was no longer flesh and blood but now a lump of carbon. The toll on the superintendent was apparent from the very beginning. One of the reporters credited with writing the *Democrat*'s headline story the morning of the fire was John Ward, who would go on to serve as a key aide and biographer of future Arkansas governor Winthrop Rockefeller. After so many years and countless reporting duties, Ward had forgotten all of the details of the story but remembered how emotionally spent and sickened Lester Gaines seemed. "He was very badly shook up. He wasn't thinking straight."[5] But how could it be that nobody was there to unlock a door?

With each explanation, Gaines appeared to be digging his own grave. The governor of the state was appointing himself prosecutor, judge, and jury. And in the nearly six years of Gaines's tenure as superintendent, no comparable event would have prepared

Lester Gaines in the slightest to deal with the press under these circumstances.

The lead story in the *Arkansas Gazette* on March 6, 1959, by reporter Joe Wirges, began predictably: "Twenty-one Negro teen-aged boys *trapped in a locked dormitory* [emphasis added] died in a fire." The article was a straightforward account that substantially tracked the lead story in the *Democrat* on March 5. But accompanying this article on the front page was a separate story headlined by the words, "Gaines Alters Account, Says Door Free." Gaines had told *Gazette* reporter Patrick Owens on the previous afternoon (March 5) that Wilson Hall, his fifty-six-year-old farm manager, in fact, had been in the building at the time of the fire. Gaines also told Owens that both the door to the dormitory inside the building and the front door had been unlocked "when the fire broke out." He also claimed that "at least one boy had gotten out through these two doors."

When summoned to confirm this new information, Wilson Hall told reporters that yes, "he was seated beside a large stove in the classroom which ran the length of the building." Hall claimed he had "been there since about ten p.m. and had been dozing." When he smelled smoke and saw the building on fire, Hall said he ran to the dormitory door "and tried to unlock it" but was driven back by the flames. Then he sprinted out the front door and ran to the rear of the building and "started pulling off screens.'"[6]

The source for Gaines's claim that two doors were unlocked was said to be an inmate by the name of Roy Davis. Rather than confirming these details, Davis told a reporter that when awakened by smoke he had tried to go to the front of the building to escape through the dormitory door that led into the classroom. Ahead of him was a boy named Jessie who "plunge[d] through the door but was caught by the fire. Davis claimed he then ran to the back and got out through a window, mentioning none of the fighting, shoving, and pushing described by the others. Nor did he claim he had reentered the building and saved two other boys.[7]

Though the *Gazette* ran Roy Davis's photograph on the front page, reporter Patrick Owens suggested in the piece that Wilson Hall had given the most "detailed" and "coherent" story about what had occurred. In writing the story, Owens had access to the diagram of the building and noted in the article that "the firemen had found one body in a position half out the door. Firemen thought the boy had died against the door on the inside and fell through when the door burned."

In the article, Owens voiced no suspicion that Gaines had coerced Hall into telling a story that would exonerate him. Owens, in fact, acknowledged that Gaines said he had not gotten "any details" from Hall. He noted that Gaines was "red-eyed" and near exhaustion.[8] Implicit in the article is that Gaines may have had no choice but to rely on others' accounts and any contradictions in the stories did not necessarily imply that Gaines had pressured anyone to lie for him.

Just hours later on the afternoon of March 6, the *Democrat* appears not to have interviewed Wilson Hall for its story about the fire but recited what Hall had been quoted as saying in the *Gazette*'s article that morning. Lester Gaines, however, was quoted extensively. Headlined by the words, "Gaines Says Keys Were Available," the *Democrat*'s story read in part that the superintendent "today stated emphatically that an adult with keys to the locked doors was stationed inside the dormitory which burned yesterday." Gaines added that "the adult, Wilson Hall, 56, got a door open and he and two other boys managed to get out, but when Hall tried to re-enter the building the flames were too high."

This statement by Gaines, of course, seemed to contradict what Wilson Hall had told reporters earlier. Hall had said he had not been able to open the dormitory door but, rather, had been driven back by the flames. The *Democrat* tried to get an explanation from Gaines about the contradictions in the stories he was telling. Apparently unaware that these stories still were inconsistent, the superintendent explained, "I was so shook up I didn't know what I was

saying. I should have had myself locked up where you newspapermen couldn't get to me."[9]

Yet again on March 6, Gaines and Wilson Hall gave a third version of the events, which was reported in the *Gazette* the next morning. Gaines told reporters that three persons besides himself had
keys to the building that had caught fire. Two of them were Wilson
Hall and an employee named Lee Austin. According to Gaines, at
the time of the fire Austin was at his residence about 150 yards away.
Wilson Hall, Gaines now said, had *not* been in the building with
the boys at the time the fire broke out after all but rather was in the
"kitchen of another building about a block from the dormitory." In
this version, Hall entered the building at the front and was met by
two boys running past him and out the door. Hall tried to enter the
dorm but was beaten back by the flames. He then ran around to the
side of the building to help pull boys through the two windows.[10]
Given all the contradictory stories he had told, Lester Gaines at this
moment seemed like the worst kind of political appointee, a hack
who lacked the experience, ability, commitment, and judgment
needed to run an institution. In fact, his defenders would say that
nothing was further from the truth.

Though scooped by the afternoon *Arkansas Democrat* and radio
and television since the fire had occurred during the early morning of March 5, the *Arkansas Gazette* now had the time to track
down the very first superintendent of the Negro Boys Industrial
School for a background story to include in its coverage on March
6. Reporter Bill Lewis interviewed an African American, Tandy
Washington Coggs, who had served as superintendent from 1923 to
1937. Coggs told Lewis that despite "criticism," it had been his "policy to make [the Negro Boys Industrial School] as much like an
educational institution as possible," meaning he had no intention to
make the school a prison. He explained, "We preferred to have a few
escapes rather than punish all the boys by confinement." Though
Coggs had not said so directly, he implied that the policy at one
time was not to lock the boys at the school inside a dormitory at

night. Lewis wrote that when the first facility for black males was completed in 1923, "there were 75 Negro boys under 16 confined in the state Penitentiary." The number of black adolescents in county or municipal jails or on county prison work farms was not given.

Coggs told Lewis that after fourteen years, he had been replaced by Arkansas governor Carl Bailey, who opposed having a black superintendent. Coggs was immediately hired to become president of all-black Arkansas Baptist College and at the time of the fire was working as the executive director of the Arkansas Teachers Association, the black counterpart of the white organization. Though Lewis mentioned in his story that Lester Gaines had become the Wrightsville superintendent in 1953, he had no reason to know that he was talking to the man who around 1930 had given Lester and Mary Gaines their first jobs at the school when it was still located outside Pine Bluff.[11] Nor would he have known that within the next twenty-four hours, Dr. Louis Coggs, a physician in Chicago and son of Tandy Washington Coggs, would try to save Lester Gaines's job as superintendent. And if that wasn't in the cards, Dr. Coggs was recommending his own father to again become superintendent. And finally, of course, Lewis would not have known that in the 1920s former slave Tandy Calvin Coggs had come to live with his superintendent son Tandy Washington Coggs and had taught "Mr. Gaines how to plow so that the dirt covered his strawberries" to keep them from being washed away.[12]

Lester and Mary Gaines appear as employees on the 1930 census taken at the Negro Boys Industrial School outside of Pine Bluff in Jefferson County. Ironically, Lester Gaines is listed as "night supervisor." His wife Mary Gaines is listed as an assistant matron.

Born January 3, 1910, Buddy Gaines had had a long and impressive association with the institution in Pine Bluff many years before he became superintendent at Wrightsville. Almost immediately after the fire, a registered, special delivery letter dated March 6 from an African American physician in Chicago arrived at the State Capitol. Dr. Louis Coggs had written the governor the following, in part:

"I have known Mr. Gaines all of my life, from the time that he was a student studying carpentry under my father who was a teacher at what has now become the A.M. & N College for Negroes at Pine Bluff." He remembered his father's employee for "most of the fourteen years" as "one of the most valuable, helpful and trustworthy members on my father's staff." Coggs added that he had seen Lester and Mary as recently as January at the school when he returned to Arkansas for a funeral. He wrote that if Gaines were given the resources, "I am certain that there is no man in Arkansas today, white or Negro, who is better qualified by background, training, interest and experience to perform this job."[13]

Under different circumstances, the opinion of Dr. Louis Coggs and his brothers and sisters would have counted for a great deal: their father, Tandy Washington Coggs, had proved to be an outstanding choice for the job as superintendent. As a role model for Lester Gaines, Tandy Washington Coggs was impressive, and that was not merely the opinion of his children. In the words of social worker and historian Erle Chambers, "Mr. Coggs' service to the State has long justified the board's choice of a superintendent. He is representative of the best type of negro. A college graduate skilled in the manual arts and child psychology, he has brought to his task the peculiar gift it needs. His indomitable determination to 'carry on' and the morale of his institution at once impress the visitor. There is a distinct *esprit de corps*."

Despite the usual condescending language ("best type of negro"), clearly the board, then all-white, had made an inspired choice. It wasn't, however, just the cheerful personality of the superintendent that was noticed.

He raises good food crops so that his charges may be fed a varied diet; strawberries are grown and eaten as well as sold. The place is clean and well kept. Under the merit system the boy works his way out. Salaries for officers and teachers seem too meager for good work, yet half the officers are high school or college graduates with teaching experience.

And yet two farms seventeen miles apart must be administered, and
buildings on neither are adequate to house decently the inmates.
There is no money for medical service, books, for any of the things
that go to make a school. And yet thus "making bricks without straw,"
the management can point with pride to the school's achievement. As
of December 1, 1926, 217 boys had been committed; eighty-four had
been paroled or discharged, and only six had escaped. Of the entire
number paroled or discharged, but six had been returned to any kind
of correctional institution. Besides agriculture, the boys engage in
dairying, poultry raising, carpentry, shoe repairing, laundry work and
household tasks.[14]

In fact, Tandy Washington Coggs, his wife Nannie, his father
Tandy Calvin, and their five children could have served as role
models for anyone. All five children obtained a master's degree or
higher. Granville Coggs, a graduate of Harvard Medical School, was
a radiologist and a partner in the Permanente Medical Group in
San Francisco; Louis Coggs became a family practice physician in
Chicago; Eloise Coggs was employed as a psychiatric social worker
in Los Angeles; Nanette Coggs taught special education in Chicago;
Tandy Washington Coggs Jr. served as a minister in Los Angeles.[15]
The influence of this remarkable family on both Lester and Mary
Gaines was significant, but it went both ways. The families would
become lifelong friends, though they would never have met had it
not been for Tandy Calvin Coggs, whose story began in slavery.
    Tandy Calvin was the patriarch of one branch of the Coggs fam-
ily, and his story starts with his forced migration as a child from
Coggsville, Alabama, to the western edge of the raw frontier state of
Arkansas. The boy's journey was said to be part of an eye-popping
dowry of twenty slave families made necessary by a white bride's
faded chances to make a suitable match. Eloise Coggs, the granddaughter of Tandy Calvin, remembered in 2010 that "the . . . girl
was long on money but short on looks so none of the upper [class]
married her."[16]

There were over 111,000 enslaved persons in Arkansas at the time of the Civil War. Though not challenging the number and size of holdings in the Mississippi River Delta in the eastern part of Arkansas or other parts of the South, the Arkansas River Valley and lowlands in Crawford County had become home to "several large slave plantations." By 1860 the largest slave owner in Crawford County was Kentucky-born David Arbuckle, the nephew of the commanding general at nearby Fort Smith on the Oklahoma border. Thanks to his excellent connections, Arbuckle was allowed to buy land on favorable terms from the federal government. He farmed 742 acres near the Arkansas River in western Arkansas. He owned sixty-one men, women, and children ranging in ages from sixty years to one-year old.[17]

Interviews granted by former Arkansas bondsmen from the federal Works Progress Administration (WPA) in the 1930s generally paint a grim picture of slave life, particularly on plantations. Crawford County, where Tandy Calvin was raised, appears to have been no exception. George Kye, who had no brothers and sisters, remembered that as a child that he "didn't live with mammy because she worked all the time and us children [on the plantation] all stayed in one house. It was a little one room log cabin, chinked and daubed, and you couldn't stir us with a stick. When we went to eat we had a big pan and all ate out of it. One what ate the fastest got the mostest." Four or five boys slept in the same bed. Though neither George Kye nor other enslaved persons appear to have been whipped or otherwise beaten on the Abraham Stover plantation, Kye recalled hearing the screams of slaves on an adjacent farm where the master "nearly beat them to death."[18]

The details of how Tandy Calvin Coggs negotiated the devastating conflict and the chaotic postwar period in Arkansas are a matter of guesswork and speculation. The presence of so many family members who were part of the same dowry may well have eased Tandy Calvin's slavery experiences. Tandy Calvin's grandson, Granville Coleridge Coggs, recited in 2010 the family lore that slavery for his grandfather had not been especially onerous, and besides, "That's just the way it was." According to Granville, his grandfather was taught to read and to do sums by the son of his master. Unlike most of the states in the Confederacy, Arkansas had no law making it a crime to teach slaves to read or write.

After freedom came, George Kye remained in Crawford County as did Tandy Calvin Coggs. Kye told his interviewer, "I lived about five miles from Van Buren until about twelve years ago when they found oil and then they run all the Negroes out and leased up the land. They never did treat negroes good around there anyways."[19] By the time of his interview, Kye, who claimed to be 110 years old, was living in Fort Gibson, Oklahoma. It would be more than seventy years later before historians would begin to understand that George Kye and Tandy Calvin Coggs had both been part of what has come to be known as the Catcher Riot.[20]

Land ownership was what freedmen wanted if merely judged by the eagerness with which they acquired it. Despite the fact that most people coming out of slavery were unable to read or write and had nothing but the shirts on their backs, by 1900 "11,766 black farmers in the state owned all or a part of their land." Almost three-fourths were homesteads of less than fifty acres, but if the land was fertile and it was in the Arkansas River Valley, a family with enough hands to pick and chop cotton could more than survive.

In 1883 Tandy Calvin Coggs would join his fellow landowners by acquiring forty acres of "very rich agricultural land, and the most valuable in the county." This was not the idle boast of a man exaggerating the high points of his life but the conclusion of a Crawford County historian in 2010. In exchange for the sum of $180, a handwritten deed filed and recorded at the Crawford County courthouse on November 13, 1883, documents Tandy's purchase of forty acres.[21] His farm was located one mile southwest of the community of Catcher. Tandy is identified in the 1880 Census as a mulatto farmer.

At the time of the transaction, Tandy Calvin was thirty-three-years-old. His son and future NBIS superintendent Tandy

Washington was born in 1887 and would come to manhood in the nadir of race relations in the South in the late nineteenth and early twentieth centuries. Yet Tandy Washington Coggs thrived on adversity. One way or another, he was going to get an education that went beyond the eight years in the black school at Catcher. Many years later, toward the end of his tenure as president of Arkansas Baptist College, he was interviewed by Ozell Sutton, the first black reporter hired by the *Arkansas Democrat*. Tandy Washington remembered that after the cotton crop had come in every year, each family member was asked what he or she wished for.

Tandy Washington recalled that he told his father Tandy Calvin he wanted to earn someday as much as fifty dollars a month. His father told him that a "country school teacher earns that much. Why don't you wish to be like [Joseph A.] Booker [president of Arkansas Baptist College]? He owns the biggest school in the state." With this prompting, Tandy Washington is reported to have said, "That's what I wish for. I wish I could own a school."[22] The story illustrates both the ambition for his son but also the understandable ignorance of Tandy Calvin, who assumed college presidents were entrepreneurs as well as educated men.[23]

The cotton crop was good some years, bad others, and wherever he went to school, Tandy Washington Coggs would not be able to afford to go straight through. According to one family story, Tandy Washington raised "pigs to make money to go down to Arkansas Baptist." But one year "apparently the pigs got cholera and he couldn't go that year." The next year, however, "he got good results" and was able to attend. It wasn't all work and no play. In 1904 at Arkansas Baptist, he met Nannie Hinkle from Okolona in Clark County in southern Arkansas. Ten years later they would be wed. As mentioned, their marriage produced five remarkably talented and hardworking children and would last until her death in 1965.

The Ministers Institute, which became Arkansas Baptist College in the heart of the black community in Little Rock, was begun in 1884 by the "colored Baptists" of Arkansas for the purposes of "educating future African-American ministers" and also "to aid the state in making higher education available to young black men and women." Arkansas Baptist would play a major role in Tandy Washington Coggs's life.[24] But it was hardly a college and wasn't even an accredited high school in those days. From the beginning, the historically black colleges in Arkansas begun in the 1880s were severely underfunded and unaccredited.

Though he graduated as valedictorian from Arkansas Baptist College in 1910, Tandy Washington Coggs had at best a high school education. Clearly under the influence of the philosophy of Booker T. Washington, the acclaimed black leader who during his lifetime made three visits to Arkansas, Tandy managed to attend Hampton Institute in Virginia for two years, obtaining a "certificate in carpentry." Family members make it clear that Tandy Washington Coggs had the option of pursuing an academic career but pragmatically chose the more practical track.[25] Given the almost intimidating academic and career achievements of his five children, one would not doubt it.

Returning to Arkansas, Tandy Washington worked for three years at Arkansas Baptist as dean of men. Then for six years he was professor of "Trades and industry" at Branch Normal College in Pine Bluff, which had been created during the Reconstruction era in 1873 by Republicans as the one state-funded school for black higher education. Under the thumb of Arkansas governors, Branch Normal was supposed to be (but was not) fulfilling the terms of the federal Morrill Act, which mandated that colleges receiving funds would teach agriculture and "mechanic arts." In fact, the Arkansas AM&N catalogue for 1925 reveals that it was only then that graduates had received a "four-year standardized high school course, receiving diplomas as such."[26] In fact, the education provided to students at Branch Normal in 1925 appears to have been inadequate at best. Louise Thompson Patterson, who had several graduate school semesters at the University of Chicago, accepted a position at Branch Normal in 1925 and was "shocked" at "the limited formal education of her students . . . because even simple arithmetic was beyond their comprehension." Worse, the system was perpetuated. When visitors appeared, she "instruct[ed] her students to work without stopping to correct mistakes on the typewriter or book-keeping machine."

Disgusted by her own complicity in promoting the sham of "an educational institution, capitalizing on the image, but rarely delivering the reality of an education, despite their students['] eagerness to learn," she quit after two years.[27]

In 1915 a highly effective "student strike" took place at Branch Normal that resulted in the closure of the school for over six months. The students were protesting the failure of the administration to investigate the allegation by student Ophelia Wade that the superintendent of the school, W. S. Harris, a white man, had handed her a package containing a "pair of black silk stockings." Finally, Harris was removed, and an African American, Little Rock native Jefferson G. Ish Jr., a Yale University graduate who had been teaching mathematics at Branch Normal, was appointed.[28]

Jefferson Ish and his wife Marietta Kidd Ish, both college graduates, had moved to Little Rock in 1873. Prototypes of the black elite, they were highly regarded in both the black and white communities. Their son, Jefferson Ish Jr., graduated from Yale but returned to Arkansas. In 1916 Jefferon Ish Jr. hired Tandy Washington Coggs. Though thousands of Arkansas blacks were drafted in the First World War, Coggs was exempted from service because he was needed to teach black troops carpentry skills.

Coggs remained as professor of trades and industry from 1916 to 1923. In the meantime, with support from the Arkansas Federation of Black Women Clubs, social workers dealing with troubled juveniles in Pulaski and Jefferson Counties, and the white Federation of Women's Clubs, the Arkansas legislature finally created an institution for black juvenile delinquents in 1921, appropriating $15,000 to be spent on "lands and improvements." Its all-white board purchased 330 acres in the Arkansas Delta southwest of Pine Bluff in Jefferson County for $6,150.

In 1923 the board hired Tandy Washington Coggs as foreman to supervise the construction and fencing of an "industrial" institution outside of Pine Bluff for black males. Realizing Coggs's talents, the board made him superintendent. In January 1924, judges began to try committing boys to the school. The first admissions were refused because there were no funds to operate it. The new superintendent refused to accept the situation and "solicited money from various negro organizations, and the board, anticipating its revenue, accepted a number of trusty boys and used them in constructing the new buildings." July 1, 1924, was formally opening day. A two-story building complete with running water and sewers was big enough to house dormitories, a dining hall, offices, and sleeping quarters for employees.

But there was no room for Coggs and his family. As a close observer of Arkansas's "correctional institutions," Chambers followed the progress of the Negro Boys Industrial School and its first superintendent. She wrote,

> To relieve congestion $2,000 was appropriated for a home for the superintendent and his family. All work on it was done either directly by the boys over a period of many months, or by exchanging their labor to pay for skilled mechanics. Most of the inside carpentry was the work of three boys, one of whom had learned his trade in the school. The floors throughout the building are hardwood, obtained at low cost from Pine Bluff mills and laid by the boys. The house is valued at $6,500.

Grandson Granville Coggs remembered the sleeping arrangements in the new house. The bedrooms for the family were on the second floor. His grandfather had a room there as well. Granville recalled a kindly old man shuffling along but still able to plant and harvest strawberries and melons, which he obviously enjoyed.

For a boy close to his grandfather (he "was the favorite grandchild") whom he remembered as "good" and "nice" and who never raised his hand to him or anybody, life in a brand-new, ten-room, two-story house in the countryside nine miles from the town of Pine Bluff was something of an idyllic existence for a black child but with a decided difference. Granville's playmates, some as young as nine, were boys who had been sentenced to the school by county judges throughout Arkansas. Granville's sister, Eloise, born in 1923, remembers that "farming" wasn't the only thing the boys did. She remembered the school had "tennis courts for the boys" and they played baseball and went swimming.[29] Disaster struck when a fire destroyed a key building, but the superintendent rose to the occasion. Chambers wrote, "In December, 1927, the large dormitory burned with a loss of $12,500 with $4,500 insurance. To house the boys a farm was rented some distance from the original institution.[30] The older boys were transferred to it and the next year they raised $10,000 worth of cotton."

At least most of this time until probably 1937, Lester and Mary Gaines lived and worked side by side with the Coggs family, all of whom seemed to have mastered the art of getting along with whites without sacrificing their dignity. As superintendent of the black school and a former teacher at Branch Normal, Tandy Washington Coggs made certain that he was friendly with the whites who mattered. Eloise Coggs recalled that powerful Jefferson County politician and lawyer Creed Caldwell (actually, part Cherokee Indian) was on good terms with her father. Probably during the 1927 flood, "Daddy brought the boys from . . . either Moscow or Tamo . . . and saved that levee."[31]

Additionally, the family, according to Eloise, also "had a wonderful relationship with the superintendent [John Reeves] of the white school." Since the Coggs had the use of an automobile, two at one point, they picked up Reeves's two children and dropped them off at their schools in Pine Bluff before going out to the "training" school at AM&N. Eloise Coggs also recalled how much her father admired Griffin Smith, "a wonderful person," who would later serve on the Arkansas Supreme Court.

Remembering her father's time in Jefferson County, Eloise Coggs was quick to distinguish between those whites who were sympathetic to blacks from what she called "white trash." Angered by an attack on her younger brother Granville, Eloise recalled being stopped by her mother from chasing Dewey, a white teenager. She said that she was mad at her father for not taking on Dewey.[32]

Tandy Washington Coggs knew what he could do and what he couldn't, for manifestations of white supremacy were never far from the surface. The Coggs children didn't require a sit-down lesson. "It was clearly manifest how we were supposed to act. We were black and we were not white but also there was prevailing optimism that things were going to get better." Granville Coggs recalled that the message from his parents was "the way you can better yourself is by education but also it was known you had to perform better than whites if you expected to receive that which whites were experiencing. [It] was fundamental that we had to do more than what whites did to receive the benefits."[33]

But there was a line that couldn't be crossed, and sometimes it wasn't always clear where that line was if you were young. Granville remembered the occasion when his brother Tandy Washington Jr. was driving him and his sisters on the highway toward AM&N and passed a truck driven by a white who was hauling black day laborers. They were followed by the truck onto the campus at AM&N. "The driver got out of the truck and accosted my brother and hit him. Knocked him down [and] told him, 'Don't you ever pass me.'"[34] Deference was always expected from blacks and could only be waived under circumstances where whites wouldn't lose face.

It was in this environment that Buddy and Mary Gaines came to be employed at the Negro Boys Industrial School. Both forty-three, Tandy and Nannie would have easily seemed like father and mother figures to Buddy and Mary. As Granville Coggs remembered in 2010, "They were actually a part of our extended family." His parents were like that. "They took in people and embraced them. And let them know they cared for them as people."

In turn, Granville Coggs would agree with his sister Eloise's assessment that Buddy Gaines was like a "surrogate father" to him. He remembered small things: that Gaines taught him how to securely tie a box; he taught him how to use a knife without cutting himself. And Granville remembered as a five-year-old how fond he was of Mary Gaines. Every day it seemed she would sweep him up in her arms. Once he got attention by saying *he* didn't mind being hugged but that she had to quit "hugging me or it would make her husband jealous."[35] Indeed, the children of Tandy Washington Coggs would have seen more of Buddy and Mary Gaines than he did during this period. Eloise recalled that for a while she seldom saw her father, since much of the time he was with the older boys seventeen miles away.

With his training at Hampton Institute, Tandy Washington Coggs was the ideal superintendent to train black boys to acquire skills that would be useful in getting a job other than as agricultural laborer. Ultimately, that was not what the white power structure wanted. On December 16, 1930, the *Arkansas Gazette* ran an article that indicated the direction of the school. "Farming has been found to be the most profitable and satisfactory method of handling the older boys. There are now between 90 and 100 boys at the school. A greater part of the land will be planted in cotton. . . . State Board takes over 600 acre tract near Wrightsville."[36] This emphasis on farming for black adolescents was certainly the "most profitable" way to administer a prison work farm. Despite what Tandy Washington Coggs had said about preferring to commit energy and resources to education, he wasn't permitted to make decisions about what the boys would learn.

The 1934 and 1940 biennial reports by the all-white board that governed both the black and white schools are indicative of how white supremacy was implemented at those times. The Negro Boys Industrial School is conspicuous by its almost total absence from the reports. In the 1934 report to Governor J. M. Futrell, the chairman of the board, J. M. Anders, mentions the Negro Boy Industrial

School only in passing. This remarkably detailed twenty-three-page report provides a litany of "permanent" improvements made at the white school but more significantly references the fact that much of the infrastructure at the white school was in equipment designed to help boys acquire skills that would help them in the job market.

Mindful of the dire economic straits of state government in the middle of the Depression, Anders listed the most important "actual need" of the white boys' school as "a new roof" for the "trades building" which housed "all the ten thousand dollars worth of machinery" that would be ruined by leaks. The report refers to the "various trades buildings" at the white school but notes that during the Depression the state did not have the money to pay instructors. At the white school in Pine Bluff the older boys went to school half a day.

The irony in this report is that the only time the Negro Boys Industrial School is mentioned, it was cited as a model because of its farm production during 1934, grossing "more than $23,000."[37] Thus, Anders urged Futrell to allow the acquisition of an additional one thousand acres for both schools. Given his expressed belief that tenant farmers, most of whom were black, were "sub-human,"[38] and the ongoing Depression, the failure to give any details about the Negro Boys Industrial School would not have troubled him. It did not need to be stated that black males, delinquent or otherwise, weren't even at the back of the line when it came to job training. Their place was in the cotton field. White boys were provided training in "carpentry and joining work, cabinet work, glazing, painting, cement work, brick laying, wood and metal-lathe operation, blacksmithing, acetylene welding, plastering, tailoring and shoe mending."[39] The only time the Negro Boys Industrial School is mentioned in the 1940 report is when it states that the white school made 156 mattresses for it.[40]

Under Superintendent Coggs, the Negro Boys Industrial School was earning almost as much from cotton production as it cost to run the institution. Act 199 of 1937 explicitly recognizes that the "farming operations" at NBIS during the "1936 crop season were unusually productive, resulting in sales amounting to approximately $27,000, which funds were deposited in the State Treasury." Language in Act 199 stated that the state of Arkansas had spent only $29,000 to run the institution for the entire fiscal year that ended on June 30, 1937.

Unable to renew the present lease of four hundred acres near Pine Bluff, a deal was worked out to rent six hundred acres belonging to the "Henry Bros. plantation" located between the communities of Wrightsville and Woodson with immediate plans to put three hundred of those acres into cultivation. Twenty-five boys would be moved "within the next few weeks to begin work with more to be transferred later." Younger boys would remain "at the main institution near Pine Bluff."

But just when the entire Negro Boys Industrial School was to be moved to Wrightsville in 1937, the tenure of Tandy Coggs came to an abrupt and unexpected end.

CHAPTER FOUR

White Supremacy

The South . . . has tended in the past to make all of its
political decisions in terms of the single issue of race.
—**Editorial in *Arkansas Gazette*,** March 19, 1949

Diversion amounted to $4,250,000 last year.
—**Ed McCuistion,** white supervisor of Negro Education for the
state of Arkansas, reporting on the amount of dollars "diverted"
by local white school boards from black schools in 1948

Housecleaning was the order of the day. Upon taking office in 1937, a former prosecuting attorney and now the new governor, Carl Bailey, immediately began to live up to his reputation as a take-no-prisoners political operative. In April both the *Arkansas Democrat* and the *Arkansas Gazette* began to run front-page stories of an ongoing purge of board members at the (white) Boys Industrial School in Pine Bluff. On April 18, the *Arkansas Democrat* reported that the white superintendent John Reeves had angered the governor because he had recently supported a political opponent of Bailey's. Charges and countercharges flew back and forth about the condition of the white boys' school and the upshot would set a pattern for the future as superintendents of the white boys' school would be replaced with regularity by new governors. It went without saying that no black superintendent would be appointed over a white school.

Within days Bailey had replaced most of the existing board. Doing his bidding, it hired a new superintendent of the white

boys' school: Clarence Dawson, a minister from Conway in Faulk-
ner County. Within a month, Bailey's board appointed James Bass
superintendent of the Negro Boys Industrial School, replacing
Tandy Washington Coggs. A former sheriff of Mississippi County
in eastern Arkansas and a "planter/banker" friend and ally of the
governor, Bass's only institutional expertise was running a county
jail in the heart of the Arkansas Delta.

Tandy Washington Coggs's firing provoked an immediate
response. Blacks came together to protest the dismissal of Coggs by
holding a rally at the Masonic Temple in Pine Bluff. Both the *Arkansas Gazette* and the *Arkansas Democrat* ignored the protest; however, according to the *Pine Bluff Commercial*, blacks from all over
the state were incensed by the new board's action. Those attending
the rally passed a unanimous resolution that read in part, "After so
many fine things have been done for reclaiming delinquent Negro
boys, we deplore the fact that the board has seen fit to replace the
colored superintendent." The resolution called on "fair-minded and
right-thinking white citizens of Arkansas" to use their influence "to
place a Negro at the head of this institution."[1]

The new board ignored the resolution, and there is no reason
to doubt Tandy Washington Coggs's statement to the *Arkansas
Gazette* twenty-two years later that Governor Bailey had wanted
a white man in the position of superintendent of the Negro Boys
Industrial School. For more than the next decade, no thought
was given to vocational programs for adolescent black males. For
them, the plan was nothing less and nothing more than a prison
work farm reminiscent of the days of plantation slavery. Not
for nothing had the governor chosen a former sheriff from the
Arkansas Delta to run it. Dr. Gordon Morgan, who later became
the first tenured African American professor at the University
of Arkansas at Fayetteville, spent the winter of 1956 researching
the Wrightsville institution for his master's thesis in sociology.
He found that "during a substantial part of the school's history
there was not [an] organized educational program of any sort.

The 'boys'... worked long hours in the field under the supervision of armed 'whipping bosses.'"[2]

In the meantime, Buddy and Mary Gaines continued their close ties with Tandy Washington Coggs and his family. All moved to Little Rock and lived within blocks of each other in the stratified and narrow world of a small black middle class composed primarily of professors, teachers, a handful of physicians, lawyers, dentists, artisans, and the Ninth Street business community. Dr. Granville Coggs remembers participating in a play at Mt. Zion Baptist Church as a child and playing the role of Mary Gaines's son. Perhaps her favorite of the Coggs children, as an adult he on several occasions visited her in Chicago while attending meetings of the Radiological Society of North America. By then she had osteoporosis and "was not the glamorous I suppose 20 year-old I hugged."[3]

Betty Hood, a teenager who lived across the street from the Gaines family at Eleventh and Cross in Little Rock, remembers them well. By the time of the fire, Buddy and Mary had a teenaged son, Lester Jr. Betty Hood remembers that Buddy Gaines "was really, really nice." He was "outgoing.... Even if they weren't your parents, they acted like them, no matter what." Lester Jr. was "a good kid ... we were all friends. [Lester was] ... a good student."[4]

Though accustomed to making do with meager resources, Tandy Washington met his match as president of Arkansas Baptist College. Hired at a particularly low point in the school's never-ending financial struggles, Coggs over the next fourteen years was able to attract students, but like most black educational institutions, Arkansas Baptist never had the wherewithal to obtain accreditation during his tenure. In 1954 he would be fired over the accreditation issue.

In the early 1940s, perhaps sooner, Buddy Gaines taught in College Station, a mostly black community near Wrightsville in the Little Rock School District. He is remembered as a much beloved teacher at the small school that went from first through ninth grade.[5] Friendly and outgoing, with excellent contacts, Gaines was eventually hired to work at the Arkansas Department of Education in Little Rock. His mentor and supervisor there was Ed McCuistion, a white man, who was director of Negro Education for the state of Arkansas. It was through this connection that Gaines would have the opportunity to be selected as superintendent in 1953.

Mary Gaines would become a teacher at segregated Dunbar Junior and Senior High School in Little Rock. Despite the fact that black teachers at Dunbar High School were only paid a little more than half of what their white counterparts received at Little Rock Central,[6] it was fully accredited. Increasingly, black families all over the state of Arkansas looked for ways to have their children educated at Dunbar.

If you were a member of the 3 percent that made up Little Rock's black middle class and lived within a narrow corridor near the state capitol, it was more than a tolerable existence so long as one was able to ignore the Jim Crow environment that surrounded it. After all, it had been years since the John Carter lynching, and despite the Depression, the area continued to be the center of black life in Little Rock, anchored by its often rough and tumble Ninth Street business district with its restaurants, theaters, and clubs.

From 1937 until the second term of Governor Sidney McMath (1950–1952), the Negro Boys Industrial School appears to have been mostly ignored except for what it could produce in farm income, which had become almost its sole function despite inadequate funding. The refusal to appropriate money to adequately maintain the infrastructure and buildings, which endured constant use from people and animals, was evident from the beginning, and the institution as a whole immediately began to deteriorate even as Arkansas's economy began to improve.

It was not as if the state always lacked the resources to maintain the Wrightsville physical plant. Governor Ben Laney informed the public in August 1945 that because of "bumper cotton crops the state penitentiary fund has a surplus of about $500,000 which has accumulated from income." The Associated Press reported that "the governor expressed hope that these funds could be used for construction of brick buildings" because "the frame structures now used to house prisoners constituted a serious fire hazard."[7] That would eventually happen at the adult prison, but despite this opportunity to fireproof dormitories at Wrightsville, nothing was done. Boys continued to sleep in firetraps (albeit brick veneer) even as the floors began to rot under them.

Meanwhile, Governor Laney continued the practice of turning over the personnel at the white boys' school. The press observed that for some time, whenever a new governor was elected, the personnel at the school was replaced. But with the Arkansas economy growing again, significant improvements at the white boys' school were reported in the mid-1940s even as the school remained a political football. Significantly,

> considerable equipment for vocational training has been added at
> the school ... an entire new water system has been installed, and with
> adequate piping. Six fire hydrants and 900 feet of hose have been
> placed on the grounds. Hydrants and fire hose are of standard thread.
> An entire new gas heating system, including gas in the kitchen and
> cannery, has been installed. The abandoned trade school building has
> been entirely reconditioned, also the inside of the laundry.[8]

The same article noted that the boys now had a "library and a reading room and a new motion picture machine purchased with screen." The American Legion was "taking active interest in the school, especially in providing Christmas parties." No mention was made of the Wrightsville institution.

In September 1947, an editorial in the *State Press* noted that "new courses were planned at the [white] Boys' Industrial School at Pine Bluff. Sarcastically, the article applauded the addition, stating "that is fine, we want the boys in the Pine Bluff school for white boys to have everything necessary to make them better citizens. That may help keep them from lynching Negroes." S. S. Taylor, assistant editor of the *State Press*, pointedly noted that the black school "need[ed] not new courses but *some* courses" (emphasis added).[9]

◆ ◆ ◆

During Ben Laney's two terms as governor, forty years after legislation creating the first reform school in Arkansas, an effort by the legislature to fund an institution for delinquent black girls to be built on acreage at the Wrightsville school came to nothing. James Bass continued as the Wrightsville superintendent, and had the funding come through, he would have been in charge of that institution as well.

Governor Laney, who acknowledged in 1945 that "little was being done toward rebuilding the characters of the boys and girls because in the past the institutions have been operated as economically as possible," was quoted as saying the same year that "we must not let economy be primary in handling of delinquent children."[10] He apparently meant only white children.

Laney was on record as opposing "federal grants as a means to lift Arkansas' educational standards," despite the fact that Arkansas needed all the help it could possibly get.[11] In 1945 there were an astonishing 2,345 local school districts in Arkansas. The State Department of Education had advised him that it would take "an additional $16,000,000 to put the state on par with the nation's average per capita expenditure for education."[12]

One of Ben Laney's solutions in 1945 to improve the image of the state was to take a trip east "to try to destroy the unfavorable, unjust and uncalled for publicity that Arkansas and its people have been getting." Laney added that he also would attempt to "dispel some of the mistaken ideas of *our* mistreatment of the Negro" (emphasis added).

Laney signed two bills in February 1945 passed unanimously by the Arkansas legislature that effectively prohibited blacks from voting in the Democratic primary.[13] State senator John Moore of Helena in Phillips County explained that the purpose was "to secure what he terms white supremacy in Arkansas' Democratic primary."[14] In the heart of the Arkansas Delta, where blacks still outnumbered whites, there was no need to speak in coded language. Of course, the blatant acknowledgement that the stated goal of the Arkansas political establishment was to maintain white supremacy had never been news to the rest of the country.

During the first few months of 1949, at the start of Sidney McMath's first of two two-year terms as governor, a handful of whites, including the new governor, were willing to confront publicly the ongoing massive diversion of resources that was constitutionally required to be made available for black schools under the US Supreme Court's "separate but equal doctrine" of 1896. Three months into his governorship, director of Negro Education Ed McCuistion was uncharacteristically in the news. On March 27, the *Arkansas Gazette* ran an article that featured his comments about black education in the state. Headlined "Official Who Knows Says That Segregated School Facilities Fall Far Short of Being Equal," the article portrayed McCuistion as an individual who spent much of his time visiting school districts primarily in the Arkansas Delta, where the bulk of blacks resided. As the first two paragraphs of the article implied, McCuistion had no axe to grind. According to the article, he was neither "a Northerner [nor] a spokesman for any Negro organization," but a "white Southerner ... a native Arkansan," a description obviously designed to give him credibility.

Born in 1892 near Fayetteville, Ed McCuistion, son of a Methodist minister, was one of twins. Both he and his brother Fred managed to work their way through Hendrix College in Conway, thirty miles from Little Rock. Ed also took courses at George Peabody College in Nashville, Tennessee. After serving in World War I in France as an aviation instructor, McCuistion was employed as a school superintendent in the Arkansas Delta, in the town of Wilson in Mississippi County. The Robert E. Lee Wilson family owned and operated one of the largest plantations in the United States. As in most counties in the Delta, the town of Wilson had no high school for black students. Before he was done, McCuistion was on hand in 1928 to open a high school for blacks and "adjusted the school year so that daily attendance for black students tripled." In 1931 he went to work for the Arkansas Department of Education and ten years later was named director of Negro Education.[15]

Eloise Coggs remembered Ed McCuistion from the days her father was superintendent, and so it is likely that McCuistion's first contact with Lester Gaines would have occurred during a visit as far back as the 1930s in Pine Bluff. McCuistion told the reporter that "he had never visited any local, sizable school unit in the state where facilities and the school program for the two races are equal."[16]

Because of his position, McCuistion knew better than anyone that Arkansas whites did not intend for blacks to receive their fair share of resources under the Supreme Court's separate but equal doctrine. Left unsaid was that after decades of routinely cheating blacks, white Arkansans were beginning to get steady pressure from inside and outside the state to equalize school funding. By 1949 four lawsuits brought by blacks to equalize funding were pending in the federal courts of Arkansas.[17] Through litigation, blacks had successfully forced states to open their doors to them in higher education. Rather than futilely litigating the issue, Arkansas began to allow a handful of native blacks to attend its professional and graduate schools.

Diplomatically, McCuistion claimed the state in recent times had never spent so much on "Negro education" as the present, but it wasn't in any way enough to catch up. Not counting construction costs, which he estimated at $7 million to $10 million dollars, it would cost the then mind-boggling sum of $4,158, 850 on a yearly basis to provide equal funding for black education.

On a district level, the "worst differential" in the state was in Crittenden County in the Delta. The article about the disparity in funding between Arkansas's white and black schools was no throwaway filler. In fact, it was part of an effort to equalize funding for black education, spearheaded by one of the South's most gifted writers.

In September 1947, South Carolinian Harry Scott Ashmore, only thirty-one-years-old at the time, had accepted a job as an editor at the *Arkansas Gazette* and was quickly promoted to executive editor. Ashmore had most recently been editor of the *Charlotte Observer*, had studied at Harvard on a Nieman Fellowship and had served in World War II.

Ashmore found kindred spirits in Sid McMath and his education department. Perceived to be far more liberal on the issue of race than he actually was, Ashmore approached the future unemotionally and with characteristic self-confidence. "The key to today's dilemma does not lie in attempting to change the white attitude by moral persuasion," he would write in his book *Epitaph for Dixie*, published in 1957, "but in re-ordering our institutions to meet the legitimate demands of the minority group." Even after the *Brown* decision in 1954, Ashmore would argue that its logic did not necessarily require integration. What was needed, he claimed, was a scrupulous adherence to the principle of "separate but equal." If that were done, Ashmore argued, the South could be said to have met its duty to its black population. In any event, if change, he wrote, must come, it would be measured in "generations" while blacks "upgraded" themselves.[18]

Thus, it was not by coincidence that education was the major topic on the agenda for the 1949 Arkansas Social Work Conference held at the Hotel Marion on April 4 and 5. The keynote speaker was McMath's new commissioner of education, A. B. Bonds, whom McMath had persuaded to give up a prestigious job at the Atomic Energy Commission to come home to help his native state. Ashmore made certain that a reporter from the *Arkansas Gazette* was present to give Bonds's speech front-page coverage.

Clearly, the conference was a highly orchestrated event to try to build support for the state of Arkansas's taking responsibility for equalizing funding for its black schools. As chairman of the conference, McCuistion presided and made the case with Bonds that money for black schools was being "diverted" to white schools on the local level. At one point, McCuisition even interrupted his boss to say that the "diversion amounted to $4,250,000 last year," which in 2015 would be equivalent to almost $42 million.[19]

Giving the keynote address at the conference, Bonds explained that this diversion of funds was not occurring at the top. The Department of Education was distributing money on an equal basis for black and white schools. "Diversion occurs on the local level," he said, meaning that the elected boards in each school district that doled out money to the schools in their geographical area were shortchanging black schools to the tune of millions of dollars each year.

The words *theft* or *stealing* would have more accurately described what was taking place. What was arguably occurring met the definition of a criminal act—converting money or property belonging to others to one's own use. But white people in 1949 Arkansas were not of a mind to accuse each other publicly of stealing money from blacks. Nor is there any evidence that whites were willing to think of their actions as stealing. Had they been willing to do so, it would have opened the state's entire racial history for scrutiny.

But lest anyone miss the point of the conference, Bonds told his audience, "If we are in bad shape in our white schools, we are in scandalous condition in our Negro schools. . . . I support the view expressed last night by Congressman Brooks Hays. If we are to have separate school facilities we must act in a Christian manner."[20]

It was an interesting application of logic. In Arkansas's past, Christianity had justified slavery; now, Christianity was going to justify segregation. The introduction of religion and morality could have been troubling at the conference had his concerns been taken seriously. It would be near the end of his life that Brooks Hays publicly confessed that as assistant Arkansas attorney general in the 1920s, "he knew in one case that $9,000 earmarked for a black school was given to a white school, [but] he let it pass because he knew that to challenge the decision would jeopardize his own budding political career."[21]

Though the obligation not to steal was hardly a new wrinkle in the Judeo-Christian ethic, during the conference the definition of morality was altered greatly by Congressman Hays, who titled his speech, "The Moral Basis for a Civil Rights Compromise [in Congress]." According to Hays, "These issues should be settled once and for all, not on a basis of political expediency, but on a basis of what is right and just."[22] Responding to civil rights proposals in Congress with what he called the Arkansas Plan, Hays told his conference audience that what was "right" and "just" meant the following: (1) all talk about ending school segregation in the South must cease since there was not yet a bill before Congress anyway; (2) the South (meaning white people) should first be allowed to take the initiative to repeal the poll tax and antilynching legislation; and (3) any fair employment legislation must lack enforcement provisions but would be "educational" in nature.

How his plan actually equated with morality and Christianity Brooks Hays would not have been able to explain. Already some Christian denominations had begun to call for an end to discrimination. On paper, for example, there was no question about what the Methodist Church believed about racial segregation. The resolution printed in the 1948 *Book of Discipline* could not have been more pointed: "The principle of racial discrimination is a clear violation of the Christian belief in the fatherhood of God, the brotherhood of man, and the kingdom of God, the proclamation of which in word and life is our gospel. We therefore have no choice but to denote it as unchristian and to renounce it as evil. *This we do without equivocation.*"[23]

◆ ◆ ◆

Sidney McMath's two administrations were defining moments in Arkansas civil rights history. After a successful legal challenge, McMath did not futilely continue to resist black participation in the Democratic Party as his predecessor had done. In his closing speech to the Democratic state convention, McMath welcomed blacks into the fold, saying, I'm proud, and I know you are proud . . . [that the Convention] . . . has said the Negro citizen is entitled to the rights and privileges of Party membership."[24]

Setting a markedly different tone in race relations, McMath was able to get out of the Arkansas legislature a significant increase in funds for Arkansas AM&N, making it possible for the only black public college in the state to gain accreditation. Despite opposition, he appointed the first black to its board. He also arranged for the state of Arkansas finally to begin operation of the Negro Girls' Training School.

What, in part, prompted Hays, Ashmore, and the McMath administration to engage in any degree with civil rights issues was that by the 1940s, the three branches of the federal government were making serious noises about the need for change. In fact the South, which had mostly been left alone to deal with its "Negro problem" since the end of Reconstruction, was again under siege. At this moment in history, the "outside forces," surprisingly, were being led in the executive branch not by an eastern radical descended from fire-breathing abolitionists but instead by a former haberdasher from Missouri, a state on Arkansas's northern border.

Though modest about his abilities, Harry Truman had no trouble making up his mind. After all, he had given the order to drop two atomic bombs on civilian populations in Japan that had changed, perhaps forever, life on earth. Now leader of the "free world," Truman and leaders in Congress like Hubert Humphrey, who were pushed hard by blacks' civil rights groups and their white allies in the North, were arguing for a number of federal measures inimical to the majority of white southerners. These included antilynching legislation, a repeal of the poll tax, creation of a Fair Employment Practices Commission, desegregation of interstate travel, desegregation of the armed forces, home rule for the District of Columbia, and a permanent civil rights commission.

Prophetically, nothing came of the education conference. Within days, the State Board of Education rejected McCuistion's proposal, "which would have required all schools in a district, Negro and white, to meet accrediting standards before anyone could be accredited." As in the past, the state board responded by doing nothing more than direct the Department of Education to send out a letter to "all school districts officials urging serious and immediate efforts at equalization." As noted by Ed McCuistion, this was a solution that had accomplished nothing in the past and would accomplish nothing in the future.[25]

Sid McMath, a decorated marine war veteran and former prosecuting attorney whose main credential was temporarily abating corruption in his hometown of Hot Springs, could afford to get out in front of his constituency only so far. McMath did not advocate ending segregation; if he had, he could not have been elected governor. In fact, in his speeches to Arkansans, he sounded much like a man who was passionate about states' rights. But the tone of his racial rhetoric was light years different from that of most other southern politicians, and so were his actions. McMath took the risk of not using race as a political weapon in his campaigns, which he acknowledged later could have cost him his first election for governor.[26]

The state finally began to operate an institution for black delinquent girls during his first year in office. For the preceding twenty-nine years, African American Floyd Brown and his wife Lillie had run a private, nondenominational, coed school, the Fargo Agricultural School, on twenty acres of land near Brinkley in Monroe County. A Tuskegee graduate and disciple of Booker T. Washington, Brown had his students attend classes half a day. The rest of the time was spent learning practical skills (boys learned "carpentry, electrical wiring, plumbing . . . built bookcases, porch swings, and wagon beds"); girls learned home economics. Though successful for many years, economic difficulties necessitated Fargo's sale. Under McMath's leadership, the state purchased the land, buildings, and equipment at Fargo and with an initial board composed of both blacks and whites started the school for black female adolescents.[27]

Unfortunately, McMath did virtually nothing for the Negro Boys Industrial School except appoint a black superintendent. On March 26, 1952, a five-person "committee for Study of State Training Schools" from various departments of state government visited the institution and its "newly appointed" superintendent, John Rawlings. Ed McCuistion was a member of the committee and made the following observation:

> I found myself somewhat depressed after returning home and thinking, here are 60 young boys, many of them with as much promise as the average youth in the homes and communities over the state. I actually felt that in some cases these boys are worse off in the institution than they might be back home where organized community enterprises might give them better opportunities to reconstruct their lives and re-fit themselves for better citizenship. I certainly feel that Arkansas should take steps as soon as possible to improve the experiences these 60 boys are having while wards of the state.[28]

What the committee found on this brief visit was that forty-six of the boys were receiving no education at all. "This is a large farm and requires a great deal of labor, much of which is done by the boys." The fourteen youngest boys were taught by the wife of the superintendent. McCuistion noted that "interviewing the boys I found a keen desire of boys in bricklaying, agriculture, mechanics, bus drivers, and guidance."[29]

The committee, which also included a physician and the head of the Welfare Department, commented on "the great shortage in personnel in handling boys in the dormitories."[30] No number of employees was given. The committee reported that there was "no regular organized recreation program. Have a picture machine and a work shop but no teacher."[31] The report noted that "feeding good on allowances available. Clothing woefully short and dirty. Laundry services seemingly limited. . . . There were few sheets or pillow cases. The mattresses appeared to be worn and soiled. No spreads other than army blankets were on beds."[32] A future board would discover there was no laundry equipment.

As to the physical plant, "the buildings are adequate but are in a very run-down condition. All the buildings need paint, floors and windows need repairing."[33] The health of the boys was commented upon. "Noticed two boys apparently sick, who were not in the infirmary—one in bed in the dormitory. No mental tests are given. . . . The Committee found that the great need is more staff for better training and supervision of the boys."[34]

There were two different views of the newly appointed superintendent. "He is evidently a little unsure of himself and is feeling his way. . . . Another report described Rawlings as "well prepared with good reputation. Needs some administrative assistance."[35]

CHAPTER FIVE

How Things Work

The entire building was a disgrace to the human eye. . . . There had been a fire in this
building the night before and the superintendent stated the boys were locked in this trap.
—Report in 1952 of an all-black inspection team at Wrightsville

The two-term reform administration of Sid McMath had gone
down in flames the previous year as a result of allegations of fraud
in the state's highway program, but as a career employee at the
Department of Education, Ed McCuistion was in a position to have
some input with the new administration in 1953. Since, as previously
mentioned, Lester Gaines worked for him, McCuistion would have
had his eye on him as a potential replacement for John Rawlings as
superintendent at Wrightsville when Francis Cherry became governor in January.

Francis Cherry already had a strong interest in child welfare.
Having been a state court judge with jurisdiction over family
law, Cherry felt more comfortable in that area and, when given
the opportunity, gravitated to it during the hapless administration of this incompetent politician. How this issue presented itself
to Cherry was not, incidentally, a textbook example of how class,
paternalism, state government, and white supremacy intersected.

In the fall of 1953 Cynthia Rushing, a Little Rock native and
social welfare major at the University of Arkansas at Fayetteville,
made a bus trip with her class and professor to institutions over
the state. These included the tuberculosis sanatorium at Booneville,
the state prison at Cummins, the white boys industrial school at

Pine Bluff, and the school at Wrightsville. What she encountered at Wrightsville "horrified" her. "There were holes in the walls," she remembered fifty-seven years later. In the dormitory were metal beds with no sheets, and it was "cold." The room "had a hanging wall heater that didn't work." As far as activities, "there was nothing for them to do. . . . They probably worked in the fields. That was probably their recreation," she guessed correctly.

Afterwards, Cynthia got off the bus in Little Rock to visit her parents for the weekend. By 1953 Scott and Mary Rushing had come a long way from the Depression. In the southern Arkansas town of Arkadelphia, Scott had owned a cleaning and pressing business that couldn't survive the economic collapse. They moved to Mary's hometown of Paragould. They had first met in college at the University of Arkansas at Fayetteville in 1927 but had dropped out after a year. In Paragould, Scott "started selling road graders for J.D. Adams Roadgrader Company."

Relocating to Little Rock with a partner to continue the business, Scott necessarily became interested in politics, since county judges had authority over roads, and county roads always needed maintenance. Scott did well financially and involved himself in numerous philanthropic causes. He helped to raise large sums of money for Catholic High in Little Rock, the Newman Center at the University of Arkansas in Fayetteville, and War Memorial Stadium. He was also a big supporter of Francis Cherry, who would become governor in January.

Incensed over the conditions at the Wrightsville school, Cynthia challenged her father to "put his money where his mouth is" and do something about the situation there. That Christmas, Cynthia and Scott took candy to the boys at Wrightsville, and her father got to see the conditions for himself.[1]

Though Cynthia remembers that she challenged her father to speak with the governor about Wrightsville, Scott Rushing may have taken a less direct but possibly more effective route. On February 2, 1953, in the middle of the legislative session, Ellis Fagan, one of Pulaski County's state senators from Little Rock, wrote Governor Cherry a letter recommending that Rushing be named chairman of the newly created separate board for management of the Wrightsville institution. He reminded the governor of a newly passed bill—"that two of the five-member Board shall be members of the Negro Race."[2] The bill had passed both chambers and would be on his desk shortly. Rushing had obviously communicated the details of the Christmas Day visit. It was understood by this time that the purpose of creating a separate board was for Wrightsville to receive some badly needed attention.

Fagan also had other constituents interested in the conditions at Wrightsville who visited the institution that January while the legislature was in session. This self-appointed group of black men was headed by Charles Bussey, who was gaining attention in the African American community in Little Rock as a political activist.[3] In a detailed, nine-page report that included recommendations for a rehabilitation program that was circulated to members of the legislature and the governor, Bussey's committee found that in the store room,

> meat was being eaten by rats; dirty bed mattresses were being stacked around the meat, which was very unsanitary.... We went to the boys' dormitory no. 1. This building was as filthy as any place we had ever seen ... the pillows were black and greasy.... The entire building was a disgrace to the human eye. Boys' dormitory no. 2, for smaller boys, was in the same condition as no. 1, except that the boys had soiled their beds. *There had been a fire in this building the night before; and the superintendent stated that the boys were locked in this trap* ... no recreational facilities.... One large boy, was in charge of the smaller ones in the class room.... Forty boys, not one clean one in the building, had on clothes too dirty for any human to wear.... Finally we visited the laundry.... To our astonishment there were no laundry facilities whatsoever. The boys were beating the clothes, putting them into old pots.... All in all, as for management, we found the boys' Industrial School at Wrightsville, Arkansas, to be in a deplorable condition.[4] (emphasis added)

It was not likely a coincidence that this all-black inspection team included Buddy Gaines, nor that Bussey would recommend shortly thereafter to the governor that Gaines replace Rawlings. Because of the eventual outcome, one might assume that it was Ed McCuistion who suggested to Gaines that a new inspection of the Wrightsville institution was in order, but it was also well-known that the activist segment of the African American community had been vitally interested in the welfare of the boys since its creation.

The outrage expressed in the report over the physical appearance and living conditions of the boys simmered beneath the surface of polite interracial discourse in 1953, but the wholesale lack of human dignity was clearly a severe affront to the pride of the black Arkansans who inspected the school. The anger never spilled over into an accusation against any specific person, that is, a white person.

Besides its chairman, two individuals bear particular mention. One was Earl Davy, who over the years worked off and on as a photographer for L. C. Bates and the *State Press*. The other, as indicated, was Buddy Gaines. On February 11, Bussey followed up the January report with a letter to Governor Cherry recommending that the "State Education Commissioner . . . give L. R. Gaines a years [sic] leave of absence to head the institution and perfect those parts of the rehabilitation program that are needed at the school."[5]

Before the session ended that winter, the legislature also passed Act 511 of 1953. It increased the total number of teachers at the school to five, including an "industrial art" teacher.[6] It was the first indication that whites truly saw the school as anything but a prison farm whose mission was to remain as self-sufficient as possible. Yet at the same time, there was no urgency coming from the governor's office about dealing with the awful conditions.

Even as poor a politician as Cherry would have realized he had a winner of an issue within hours of his visit to the Arkansas Boys (White) Industrial School in Pine Bluff in June 1953. A letter to him complaining that some of the boys were being used to do chores for the mayor of Pine Bluff got his attention, but it was his attention to the plight of children who had done nothing to warrant exile to a reform school that won him some decent press and kudos from constituents.

During a visit, an indignant Cherry "rescued" three of the children by demanding the state find foster homes for them. The headline of the statewide *Arkansas Gazette* on June 11, 1953, trumpeted, "Cherry Demands Boys School Cleanup." The governor fumed against "the idea of sending a child to that place when his only fault was that he had been abandoned or neglected!" Continuing, the governor said that he "was not at all pleased with the over-all picture at the Boys School." There was little recreation being provided, "and the older boys' quarters were a mess." Cherry said that he didn't know what he could do, "but we sure can clean it up."

He vowed to bring "30 or 35 women from over the state" to visit the school with him, saying that women wouldn't tolerate the conditions at the Pine Bluff school. The publicity resulting from the story resulted in a rare public relations bonanza. Before he was done, approximately two hundred white women toured the school with him.

Shortly after his visit to the white boys' school in Pine Bluff, Cherry finally toured Wrightsville with his director of public welfare, A. J. Moss, and members of his department. Besides Bussey's report, Cherry also had available the 1952 report by the previous welfare director under the McMath administration. The conditions had not changed in the five-month interval since the visit of Gaines and the other members of the committee.

Titling his report of the visit to Wrightsville "Plans for Cooperation with the Negro Boys Industrial School," Moss and his employees counted seventy-six boys in the institution. Though there were positions for twenty-four full-time employees, there were only thirteen at work the day of the inspection. According to this report, the school owned 2,300 acres, 400 of which were in cultivation. Major crops were corn (125 acres), cotton (120 acres), and beans (70 acres). Along with other previously documented problems, "the

Superintendent of the school had no social records or case histories on the children which means that a great deal of case work will have to be done to develop the available resources for placement of the boys." Moss concluded that "nothing is done ... towards rehabilitation."

Particularly disturbing were the interviews with younger boys between the ages of fourteen and ten years old. Of these nine children, "they had two things in common. They were all from broken homes and all were charged with theft. These charges ranged from stealing bicycles, bee bee guns to theft of money."

Once a boy was at Wrightsville, it was sometimes difficult to release him after the arbitrary minimum of six months because a place had to be found in the community or with relatives. The report observed that "the school has no money to pay for the boys' bus fare back home, and lack of this money causes many delays in the return of the youths to their respective homes after they have served their time."

The farm also included "43 head of cattle, 90 head of hogs, 5 tractors, 14 mules, 4 horses." As in the other two reports, there was no mention of any vocational program. As stated, boys under fourteen were taught by Rawlings's wife.

In a conversation with the governor, Superintendent Rawlings listed his "main needs" as "a better water supply"; "repair of plumbing"; kitchen equipment, especially a new stove and ice box; "new screens on all buildings"; and "repair of flooring throughout." The report makes no mention of whether Cherry understood that the well water was undrinkable, though the boys drank it and had been drinking it since the school was moved to two miles outside of Wrightsville. Cherry surely should have suspected the water was bad since the staff brought their own water to drink. The water provided to the boys was reddish in color and appeared to have a high iron content.[7]

Though the report written by Moss is silent on the subject, apparently the administration of the school by John Rawlings did not impress Francis Cherry. In a speech in Atlanta the week after his visit to the NBIS, he told to the Georgia Big Brothers Association that "the school had atrocious plumbing, no recreational facilities, very little athletic equipment and not enough linen."[8]

Rawlings was out as superintendent within a month. His replacement was Buddy Gaines. In his defense, Rawlings, a graduate of Arkansas AM&N, had been employed, according to his wife, at the school as a counselor and apparently had little direction from anyone during his brief tenure in his new job as superintendent. In neither of the reports by the state of Arkansas did anyone even know how to spell his name correctly.[9] After he was removed as superintendent, he embarked on a career as the first black county agricultural extension agent for the state of Arkansas. He died in 1988. His wife was interviewed by historian Jajuan Johnson for the Butler Center for Arkansas Studies and somehow remembered their stay at Wrightsville in glowing terms.[10]

Buddy Gaines began as superintendent on July 1, 1953. In just over a month, at the direction of state educational commissioner A. E. "Arch" Ford, a committee of state employees from the Department of Education that also included Governor Cherry's executive secretary was offering Gaines "educational" and "vocational" consultations which took place on August 5 and 6.

On August 12, the committee met in Ed McCuistion's office in Little Rock. McCuistion, Gaines, and Rushing, chairman of the board, met with three other state employees concerned with education. Afterwards, D. E. Blackmon, assistant commissioner of education, wrote his boss (Commissioner Ford) that Rushing and Gaines "are extremely interested in establishing an educational program at this institution." On August 18, Blackman wrote Gaines, "I should like to compliment you on the business-like manner in which you are going about in setting up this program."

By August 25, Blackmon had received a letter from the governor's executive secretary, Ken Francis, acknowledging that the "plan" had been received. "I have shown the information to the Governor and

I believe he is now familiar with it."[11] The "plan" called for a total of five teachers for all ages and included vocational training in carpentry, blacksmithing, farming, and mechanics. Boys would be tested for aptitude, intelligence, and achievement. Records on all the boys would be created and maintained. Buildings at the school were to be renovated to provide classrooms and an auditorium, with desks and chairs to be provided by the state surplus property manager. An orientation with teachers was to take place once they had been hired. On paper the plan was obviously an improvement, but significantly, there was no investment in the kinds of shop equipment available at the Boys' Industrial School for whites.

In the paternalistic tradition that governed the etiquette and implementation of white supremacy, Francis Cherry meant well. He persuaded successful white businessmen, including Jack Stephens and Harvey Couch, to join a foundation to raise money to assist both "industrial schools for whites and Negroes" in creating a "recreation and rehabilitation program."[12] Rehabilitation proved beyond reach or perhaps beyond the interest of white businessmen, but enough money was raised to allow the construction of swimming pools at both facilities, and as mentioned earlier, it would be from the swimming pool that firemen would cool down the ashes of the fire.

But by locating the school in an isolated rural area, the state of Arkansas had guaranteed the worst possible outcome should a fire occur. The danger was obvious to white authorities. *Arkansas Democrat* publisher K. August Engel acknowledged as much when he wrote that "it had been discussed moving the school." But Wrightsville was apparently not important enough to justify the trouble and expense.

Paternalism masked the real needs of the school but served as a useful palliative. While blacks and whites were smiling at each other and making nice at meetings of the Greater Little Rock Urban League over racial "progress," the national NAACP had begun working with local chapters in the South to challenge discriminatory practices in public education that culminated in the seminal case of *Brown v. Board of Education* in 1954 and the litigation that has continued through the present. Daisy Bates would observe bitterly about the Urban League that it was "just a chance for niggers to sit next to whites every two weeks."[13] Yet because whites were involved, Bates had no choice but to take the Urban League seriously, even if little of substance was accomplished. Also, for the same reason she joined other organizations. It was a source of news for the *State Press*.

On May 15, 1954, the US Supreme Court announced its unanimous antisegregation decision in *Brown v. Board of Education*. Nothing between blacks and whites could ever be the same again, no matter how inconvenient it was for both races to face reality.

Though news about Wrightsville would vanish during the next year when Cherry was defeated by Orval Faubus in the Democratic primary, in an article in the Memphis *Commercial Appeal* on March 24, 1954, a reporter gave his impressions of the (white) Arkansas Boys Industrial School. He wrote that much had changed under a new superintendent. Boys at the white school were said to no longer be whipped for infractions and instead given demerits and denied a pass to leave the institution for a visit home upon accumulation of a certain number. A daily, mandatory athletic program was instituted. The staff was increased to twenty-four, and the emphasis was now on "rehabilitation rather than punishment." While this was largely traditional window dressing that occurred with the installation of each new superintendent, at least someone was paying attention. Typically, the article did not mention the institution at Wrightsville.

With the incoming Faubus administration came a new chairman of the Wrightsville board of managers. It was understood that the head of the board would be white and would have political ties to the governor, and in that respect a number of influential supporters of the governor would have filled the bill. Though Paragould in the northeast corner of the state had in its past a reputation as a Sundown Town with a history of driving out its black residents, thirty-two-year-old Union Pacific railroad employee Alfred Smith, like

Scott Rushing, his predecessor, began his tenure as chairman with a hands-on approach that promised better days ahead for Wrightsville. Clearly determined to treat his fellow board members with dignity and fairness at his very first board meeting on April 12, 1955, Smith called the meeting to order and promptly read from *Robert's Rules of Order*, surely an Arkansas first in an integrated setting. "The quorum of any deliberate assembly, unless the business rules provide for a smaller quorum, [shall be] the then majority of all the members." Two of the board members that day, Smith and African American Jeffrey Hawkins, a rising political leader in Little Rock's East End, would make up two of the three members of the board who conducted the investigation ordered by Faubus on March 7, 1959.

Smith was the voice of optimism at his first meeting. The minutes reflect that he "complimented the fine program in operation at the institution . . . and predicted a pleasant and profitable program for the Negro Boys' Industrial School." That Smith's comments about "a fine program" were obviously hyperbole was shown by two items on the agenda that were postponed for future discussion. Despite all the past comments during the previous year about the filthy condition of the boys, in April 1955 there was still no laundry and no freezer, an appliance that was "badly needed at the School for the preservation of its home-grown foods."[14]

A native of Illinois, Alfred Smith clearly had no illusions about the conditions at the Negro Boys Industrial School. A month later, at the second meeting of the board during his tenure, "the water system" at the NBIS was discussed at length." The minutes reflect that Smith invited to the meeting a Mr. P. L. Hoshall, "a water expert" who deemed the well water consumption not merely undesirable but unsafe, as a later test by the Department of Health confirmed. Naive about what could be done to correct fundamental problems such as these, the board voted to instruct Gaines "to negotiate for the installation of . . . an adequate water system, submit invitations for bids [with] the job [to] go to the lowest qualified bidder." That would take an appropriation, and during the Faubus governorship, that kind of commitment would only come years later when Faubus was fighting to delay through litigation the desegregation of the boys school.[15] Despite the initial enthusiasm of both Gaines and Smith along with the two black members of the board, changes would come either not at all or be too small to make a difference.

As previously mentioned, a master's thesis in 1956 by sociologist Gordon Morgan illustrates the fundamental problems at Wrightsville. His detailed description of the institution during the winter of 1956 suggested an all-too-familiar model found in the distant past.

Though slavery was officially dead, the prison farm atmosphere eerily mimicked some of its most degrading and brutal features. In significant ways, the job of superintendent and staff roughly corresponded to that of plantation overseers and slave drivers. "While the administration does not condone brutality in the treatment of youths, liberal use is made of the leather 'strap'. . . . Runaways almost always are whipped upon their return to the School and placed on the hardest detail."[16]

But more than punishment was at issue. Morgan wrote that "vocational education suffers greatly at the School. There is no adequate shop only a few old tools which can be used. Some agriculture and wood-working is taught but most of the training is in the form of practical work."[17]

To say that Wrightsville was not designed with the dignity of the individual in mind is, of course, an understatement. Morgan notes that one thirty-gallon hot water tank was supposed to serve a maximum of 150 children, the capacity of the school. With no laundry equipment ("two large iron kettles were used for heating water") and no institutional standard of cleanliness, the filth of the boys was guaranteed from morning to night, day in, day out. Though there was a laundress, "many boys go for days with only rags for clothes. More than half wear neither socks nor underwear during winter of 1955–1956 while this study was in progress."

During the winter, most of the older boys were not required to take a shower. Most boys did not have a "complete" change of clothes. Morgan writes, "Clean bodies are a badly neglected aspect of the process of training at the Wrightsville School." The dormitories were not equipped with lockers or boxes of any sort. Thus, it was "impossible for them to keep even such personal items as tooth brushes and paste, soap, combs, shoe polish and hair preparation."[18]

As others had done before, Morgan comments on the lack of bedding. Sheets and pillowcases were virtually nonexistent. In addition to the fact there was little or no credible vocational program, Morgan could not document an academic program for boys older than fourteen. The lack of funding, programs, and personnel for the school insured over time a mindset that inured itself to the appalling conditions that continued year after year.

But it was not only inadequate funding from the legislature that had contributed to the squalor found at Wrightsville. Young black males weren't considered worth rehabilitating. Morgan found that "during the earlier period, while the school was operated as a division of the Arkansas Boys Industrial Schools, it was generally conceived of, by members of the Board of Managers and others, as a productive agricultural enterprise, and little attention was paid to either the education or reform of the inmates."[19]

Yet in contrast to the past, Morgan did rate the current situation "to be a substantial improvement over . . . earlier conditions" at the school. Some of the "earlier conditions" that Morgan had in mind dealt with the change in accounting practices that were brought about by the legislative "reforms" in 1953. Morgan notes that until then, employees were not required to account to the state of Arkansas for any "earnings" made from the sale of farm products. Morgan observes that "at various times in the past there has been more than a suggestion of not only incompetence but also of dishonesty in the management of the school."[20] In other words, the previous accounting practices were an open invitation for persons to put money into their own pockets. Morgan writes, "It is believed that this practice encouraged mismanagement and theft by School officials. With the School operating first as a self-sustaining unit, few State appropriations had to be made aside from salaries for employees. Inquiries were seldom made into the disposition of the school's earnings."[21]

As noted, employees were given a place to stay at Wrightsville and ate for free, but Morgan found they were rarely off duty (some only one weekend per month) and received subsistence pay. Initially, the physical plant of the farm must have been imposing. Morgan counted more than thirty structures, including a "sawmill, a blacksmith shop, a cotton gin," barns, and other buildings. Yet from the date of completion of these WPA structures and renovation of existing buildings, the budgets for Wrightsville allowed for little maintenance. By 1956, as Morgan and others had noted, "All buildings on the campus are in need of extensive repairs, *particularly the boys' living quarters*" (emphasis added).

Employees had no expectations of advancement or pay raises, but there were few, if any, qualifications required for jobs. Morgan writes that

> In recent years the administrations have selected employees on the basis of interviews alone without the formality of presenting evidence of suitable training or preparation for this type of work. . . . About half of the present employees are quite elderly and have been with the School since its founding. It is evident that at least some of them, because of advanced age, cannot fully accomplish the duties and responsibilities assigned them.[22]

Employees received no sick leave or "leaves of absence," no matter how long they had been employed. Decades after its founding, there was no contract of employment, no retirement, no periodic pay raise. There was no training for employees or possibility of advancement. The average mean salary was $1,711 a year. As noted, housing, including utilities and cafeteria food, were available to the employees, who were also entitled to the staples produced by the farm.

Morgan's thesis in 1956 gives a snapshot of who the boys were and what they had done to merit incarceration at Wrightsville. Morgan found most boys were guilty of nonviolent conduct, "burglary, and truancy." He writes that "murderers and rapists are generally committed to the penitentiary. . . . A number of boys at Wrightsville have virtually grown up in the School. Of the present sample, thirty youths have been committed two or more times. The remaining forty-two boys are in their first commitment." He reports that two boys were at NBIS for homicide and two for arson.

Slightly more than half of the boys at NBIS were fourteen or younger. Two were ten years old. Morgan does not specifically mention if any of the boys at Wrightsville in 1956 had been committed simply because they had no families to take care of them. However, he was able to obtain some information about their family situation. Over half of the children at NBIS were from "broken" homes, but these were not children of "welfare" mothers. Only three of the boys reported their mother received a check from the government. Well over half of the women were employed (45), most as maids (30), which was about all black women could expect in the way of employment in this era. Thirteen boys could not give the occupation of their fathers, but of the rest, only two said their fathers were not employed. Only three fathers were listed as being "skilled laborers." Nor were these likely children of criminals. Only two of the boys reported their fathers had been in prison or a reform school. Given the fact that the mean number of siblings for Wrightsville inmates was six, and most fathers were not in the home, children easily got lost in the shuffle.

As a budding sociologist, Morgan was well versed in the existing literature on theories of criminality and thoroughly understood the significance of probation services as an "invaluable tool" in dealing with potential recidivism. The obvious features of a good probation program were that it was "individualistic in treatment, leaves the child in his home environment, and is not punitive in character and therefore free from social stigma." He writes, however, "In Arkansas cities probation services for Negro juveniles can best be described as nominal."[23]

Fifty years later Morgan, teaching at the University of Arkansas in Fayetteville, added some personal observations about Buddy Gaines. His opinion was that the superintendent was

> not very aggressive nor authoritarian. Not every employee always showed up when they were supposed to. You have to understand that in those days the whites in charge did not want you to be running back and forth to them with problems. You had to make do with what you had. . . . I recall he was very open. He didn't seem to have a lot of information. There was not much bureaucracy, no records. Wrightsville did not count for very much. Jobs were political. There was still a relationship between the prison at Cummins [the adult prison for males] and Wrightsville. You took a job because you needed a job. Gaines might have been qualified to teach shop in school. Gaines would have had to go along with the system.

Asked about Gaines's supervisory responsibilities and how he discharged them, Dr. Morgan replied, "I would say that the oversight was not all that great. I never saw any reports on what the boys were doing. Records were incomplete."

It appears that however enthusiastic Lester Gaines and Alfred Smith had been at the beginning of their mostly overlapping tenures as superintendent and board chairman, by 1956 both would have realized how little support the state government was going to give the school at Wrightsville. By then it appeared that morale was at its lowest ebb. A letter from Alfred Smith to the governor requested that two members of the board be relieved of their duties because of their inability to attend meetings. Queried if "Mr. Gaines [was] incompetent or did he simply lack resources," Dr. Morgan responded, "It may have a bit of both. Teaching school in those days paid almost as much as supervisor of an institution like NBIS. In 1956 I taught high school at Conway and was paid $2,700." Gaines earned $3,400 and received free lodging and food.

In an abbreviated telephone interview for this book, Barbara Gatlin, the daughter of Alfred Smith, spontaneously remembered Lester Gaines's surname, recalling that her father was "crazy" about Mr. Gaines and said that he thought Gaines was doing an excellent job as superintendent. For reasons never explained, she declined to comment further and refused to respond to questions by e-mail after first agreeing to do so. Another family member also declined to be interviewed.[24]

Dr. Morgan's retrospective assessment of Gaines's abilities may well have been correct, but other information during his tenure suggests a more dynamic personality. Whatever platitudes governors and the legislators uttered about the rehabilitative purposes of the Negro Boys Industrial School, its superintendent was expected to generate substantial farm income and keep expenses down.

While Gaines was administrator of the so-called school, in fact, agricultural production had never ceased being the real purpose of the institution. Responsible for the bottom line, he made the purchases and filled out the paperwork required by the state. The fact that he appears to have been treated with respect by his own board chairman and certain employees of the Arkansas Department of Education would not have signaled to him that race relations were now substantially different in the state. The Central High School Crisis in Little Rock had revealed publicly the hostility blacks encountered when they asserted themselves "too" aggressively. Whites still expected blacks to defer to them.

After almost five years as superintendent and an ongoing purchaser of farm equipment and supplies, Gaines was hardly a black teenager from the North needing to be reminded of what happened to Emmett Till. The old adage that the more things changed the more they stayed the same applied to Arkansas race relations, especially in rural settings.

Buddy Gaines's encounter with a white clerical employee at Pulaski Implement Company illustrates a facet of Gaines's personality that few would have seen. A white employee complained to the governor's purchasing agent that "sometimes there are seven or eight people in here and Gaines will come in and shove them aside and demand to be waited on and assigns us all jobs such as saying and you get me that."

Though this particular scenario is obviously an exaggeration, admittedly there was, as Gaines explained, "tension" between him and the clerk over the number of copies of purchase orders needed by the state to satisfy its bureaucracy. The dispute almost ended in a fight that could have easily escalated into a shooting.

According to Gaines, the employee, furious, had motioned as if to pick up a stool to hit him. In the account of the incident sent to Mack Sturgis, Gaines wrote, "If [the employee] had picked up that stool to hit me, I was going to shoot him." Gaines might well have been serious, for he had a permit to carry a gun that he kept in his truck. He later telephoned the Pulaski Implement Company to find out who had reported him to the police. Gaines acknowledged that others had treated him well at Pulaski Implement but from then on he would take his business to Pine Bluff.

A less dramatic but possibly more telling incident occurred in 1958. A letter to Governor Faubus from Clara Gerard, a white woman who served as postmistress at Wrightsville, reads,

> I feel that this is a must—Last night January 12th, three boys (or more) from the Negro Boys Industrial School broke into our store again, broke one plate glass window and one glass [window] in the post office entrance, taking money and tearing up in general. As I'm sure you know, your superintendent does not reside there [on the grounds of the NBIS] and these boys are allowed to run at random. They work here and there, are allowed too many privileges.

Gerard continued in the same vein, writing that the superintendent had not made full restitution for the damages the last time and there had been a dispute over a tractor he had bought. Gerard claimed the tractor was damaged. She admits however, that she "took this up with Mr. Sturgis, your purchasing agent, but to no avail."[25] Obviously, there was another side to this, but the outcome is not known. It does not appear that Governor Faubus responded by mail to her letter, but he or someone in his office may have called her.

Certainly, it put the governor on notice that there was reason to believe that Lester Gaines might not be spending his nights on campus. Later, this information would become useful to Faubus.[26]

CHAPTER SIX

Not Business as Usual

Mr. Gaines is one of the finest men I have ever known
and he certainly has these boys' interests at heart.
—**Althea Wood Martin**, day supervisor over "large" boys' dorm, answering questions
at the hearing conducted by the Wrightsville Board, March 7–9, 1959

White men questioning blacks about their alleged bad behavior or what they knew about the alleged behavior of other blacks is a tradition as old as slavery in Arkansas, and few interrogations would have been feared more. Some of the most vicious and documented accounts of sustained torture had occurred during the aftermath of the Elaine Race Massacres of 1919. Claiming fear of a "revolt" by blacks in the Arkansas Delta, members of the US military, planters, and county and local officials in Helena spared no efforts to make sure that blacks gave up information, accurate or otherwise, that conformed to their desired version of events.[1]

Much more routine, individual black Arkansans have been taken into police stations for questioning and have emerged with injuries or in some cases not at all.[2] One of the most detailed and thorough examinations of the futility of black Arkansans seeking justice against police misconduct in Arkansas history involved the police shooting of twenty-four-year-old Carnell Russ in the Star City police station in 1971. Pulled over with his family in the car by the state police for an alleged traffic violation, Russ was shot in the head less than an hour later inside the Star City jail.[3] He never recovered consciousness and died in a hospital the next morning.

Under Wrightsville board chairman Alfred Smith, there were no forced confessions in the investigation of the NBIS fire. Part of the difficulty for investigators is not that questioning took place under draconian conditions, but that only a portion of the written transcript or transcripts of what was called the confidential hearing or other official reports appears to have survived.

Though Alfred Smith told reporters on March 10 that twenty-three witnesses had been called behind closed doors beginning on Saturday and again on Monday, only a single self-contained document setting forth questions by him and answers given by fourteen Wrightsville employees has been located. This document also contains the conclusions reached by the board, possibly suggesting that other interviews were not transcribed or recorded.

The content of any conversations and instructions, if any, the governor might have had with his board chairman, Alfred Smith, and two black members prior to the hearing is unknown; however, the stated intent of the questioning is set forth in the first paragraph of the document: "This investigation is called . . . to develop the facts and place responsibility in connection with the burning of the teenage boys' dormitory at the Negro Boys' Industrial School."

The caption of the twenty-seven-page transcript of the hearing conducted over two days by three members of the NBIS board gives the location of the hearing as the Negro Boys Industrial School, Wrightsville, Arkansas, and the date as March 7, 1959; the label "confidential investigation" was applied. Present were Alfred Smith, chairman of the school's Board of Directors, and board members J. C. Hawkins and A. E. Woods. The identity of the individual who typed the transcript is not disclosed.

Witnesses were not required to give an oath as would have been the case in a legal proceeding conducted by lawyers pursuant to the Arkansas Rules of Civil Procedure. Alfred Smith began by stating that the purpose of the board in examining employees was to allow each to be called individually and permitted to state whatever relevant facts were in their possession. Unfortunately, the names of the other nine individuals questioned were not revealed.

Creating even more difficulty for future investigators is the fact that repeated searches by a trained archivist and others have failed to turn up official investigations ordered by the governor to be conducted by the Arkansas State Police, which included a report of the state fire marshal. Nor is it clear at what point the board was given access to these investigations. Finally, deaths and impaired memories have taken their usual toll in the ability to supplement the written record.

It appears that at this juncture that all the board was responsible for was questioning the employees of the school. In retrospect, whatever private instructions were given, if any, by the governor, one could conclude from newspaper accounts that Faubus was taking aim at Buddy Gaines. Assuming the board had followed the stories in both papers, Lester Gaines was to be a target of the investigation, whether the governor had said so directly or not.

The governor had no apparent reason to doubt the loyalty of Alfred Smith, the chairman of the Wrightsville board. It wasn't Smith who was sounding off to the press about how terrible conditions were at the school. In fact Faubus would have had no reason to doubt the outcome of any investigation. His superintendent kept changing his story every time he told it. All that was really needed to do was to put all the contradictions side by side, and Gaines's guilt would appear obvious.

The first employee to "testify" was Mrs. E. Givan, who functioned as receptionist and secretary/bookkeeper. Thirty-one-years-old, she had been employed at the school for three years. She said that she and her husband (not an employee of the school) lived on campus with their two children. They received the use of a house and utilities at no cost. Employees were provided vegetables produced on the farm in season. Mrs. Givan stated "she had the utmost respect and high regard for the Superintendent."

Smith asked her if she was under any pressure from the superintendent, or any member of the board. Givan answered, "Absolutely not." Nor, she said, was she told in advance that an investigation was being held. The picture of Gaines began to change with Ms. Givan's statement of her duties. Her responsibility was to type up a work schedule every Monday outlining each employee's duties for the week. She was assigned to give a copy to each employee and then attach a copy on the office bulletin board.

Sounding very much like a lawyer, Smith had her hand over a copy of the schedule for the workweek starting March 2, 1959, and marked it as "Exhibit A."[4] Smith had the witness hand him a list of employees who resided on campus and again had the list identified as an exhibit. Only the list of employees has survived.

Smith asked Givan if she knew if employees were given the responsibility of staying with the boys on the night of the fire. Ms. Givan replied that she knew that two were assigned to this particular building. She identified them as "Mr. Austin and Mr. Hall" and said they would have had keys to the front door of the older boys' dorm.

Givan told Smith she was first called by the nurse, Mabel Fleming, who told her the big boys' dorm was burning down. She stated that she told her husband to run over to the superintendent's house but then added she called Gaines herself. She then followed his instructions to call the fire department. In retrospect, the mystery of whether Gaines was on campus would not be solved by her testimony, for she does not reveal whether she called him at his house in Little Rock or at the house provided for him on campus. Assuming Givan was telling the truth, she must have thought the superintendent had spent the night on campus or she would not have sent her husband over to the superintendent's residence. Perhaps she changed her mind and called him because it was obviously quicker.

While prior investigators, both black and white, have painted a dismal portrait of the operations of the school, the employees naturally saw their environment in a different light. They didn't understand themselves to be part of a prison farm that did nothing but work the boys, nor was that the case while Gaines was superintendent. For example, Givan stated she liked her job because it also allowed her to do counseling and teaching Sunday school and dramatics.

Smith asked whether she knew that Wilson Hall and Lee Austin were in the building at the time of the fire. Givan said she didn't know but to another question answered that according to her work chart they were supposed to be.[5]

Employee after employee corroborated Givan's testimony about a posted work sheet outlining that week's duties. Althea Wood Martin stated there were two copies—one on her bulletin board and another on the office bulletin board. As house directress for the older boys, Martin worked in the building that was destroyed by the fire. She stated that she worked with Hall and Austin "during the day, and I knew that they were supposed to take care of that building and the boys in it." Asked twice why she was certain Hall and Austin were assigned to this building on the night of March 4 and the morning of March 5, Martin responded that when an employee was gone the superintendent assigned someone to take his place. She said that this always occurred during her four years on the job. "I just *know* he had someone to fill Mr. Banks' place." As Givan had done, she fiercely defended Gaines: "Mr. Gaines is one of the finest men I have ever known and he certainly has these boys' interests at heart."[6]

School nurse Mabel Fleming told Smith the reason she knew Austin and Hall were responsible for checking on the boys during Banks's illness was because she had overheard the superintendent inform Mrs. Givan to send for Mr. Hall and Mr. Austin because he wanted them to fill in for Mr. Banks.[7] More than fifty years later, an interview with Ms. Fleming was deemed unreliable due to problems with her memory.[8]

Trades and Industrial teacher Bernard Hallum Childress, who was one of Gaines's first hires upon taking the job on July 1, 1953, not only claimed that he heard Gaines assign Hall and Austin Banks's duties after he went to the hospital but that he saw them perform them.[9] Unfortunately, he did not describe what these duties were.

Hired in 1958, Winton Mattison, who was thirty-five years old at the time, said his position at the school was working in the shop. Mattison said that he was familiar with the schedules handed out by the superintendent each week and that he was aware Austin and Hall were going to take over for Banks.[10] Finally, Mattison said that Gaines, Hall, Austin, Fleming, and Childress were all present at the scene of the fire when he arrived. By that time, flames were all around the building.

Luther Fleming, who held the position of assistant farm manager and mechanic, told the board that he too was familiar with the work chart issued weekly by the superintendent, and that he saw Hall and Austin performing these duties. He also testified that at times he had supervised the "big boys" dorm and that as part of his duties he would be required by Gaines to stay the entire night after he got the boys to bed. Asked if it was normal to have the door locked, he said it was.[11]

Though Gaines and Wilson Hall had already given contradictory statements to the Little Rock papers about their whereabouts and actions during the night of the fire, Hall gave yet another version under questioning by Smith. Employed as the farm manager for the previous twelve months, Hall said he got up every morning at three during this period: "The Superintendent instructed me to check on the building and the boys—to go around and see how the boys and the building were getting along, and to check on the man. It was not my direct responsibility, but I was told to check on the man [Austin] in charge. I was supposed to make these checks every night until Mr. Banks returned."

Hall claimed that Austin was always on duty when he went by at nine and three. He stated that he was the first person to the dorm: "When I got there and saw this, I couldn't get through the door. I ran round to the back and began tearing screens off the window. There were no other employees." Asked when he saw Austin, he replied, "It was sometime after I had gotten there. I went over to the office to help lay planks so the fire truck could get to the pool." Like all the other employees, Hall denied that anyone had talked to him about the hearing.[12]

Though Wilson Hall had by this time given four different versions of his whereabouts during the fire, for some reason Smith did not confront Hall with his contradictions. Not a resident of central Arkansas where the papers were widely circulated, Smith appears not to have read or at least not to have read closely the ever-changing accounts given by Gaines and Hall in either the *Arkansas Gazette* or the *Arkansas Democrat*. As mentioned, according to his daughter, Smith thought highly of Gaines and may have already been predisposed to believe him even before the other employees testified for him.

Lillian Hall, the wife of Wilson Hall, said that on the morning of the fire her husband had left their house "between 3 or 4, I guess." She said that her children were at home. She ran the "laundry" for the school.

SMITH: "Prior to 3 AM, where was your husband?"

HALL: "At home."

SMITH: "Did your husband advise you that he was detailed to supervise the Big Boys' Dorm?"

HALL: "I don't know."

SMITH: "You had no conversation as to his specific duties?"

HALL: "No."

Almost fifty years later, the children of Wilson Hall would challenge the entire account of the whereabouts and duties of their father.

Though Lee Austin's name had never been mentioned previously by Gaines, Wilson Hall, or anyone else in the numerous articles about the fire, Austin was now a key witness. Austin had been livestock supervisor at the school for two years. His wife was the cook, and they lived on campus.

Austin said, "I was in the building until about 3 o'clock when the lights went off, and I went home across campus to get a flashlight to check on the lights. . . . I was in my house looking for a flashlight. Then I heard someone yelling and saw a big light." Austin further said, "Mr. Hall had been by a couple of times, I heard him talking to some of the boys." Austin also admitted that he left no one in charge. Crucial to his position was the reason for leaving the boys. According to him, the lights were off in the dorm, "It was raining, storming and real windy. I went to get a light to try to see how to get the lights back on."

SMITH: "You were taking 20 to 30 minutes to go approximately 100 yards to get a flashlight?"

AUSTIN: "Yes, sir, but I never did find it. I was hunting for it but I never did find it."

SMITH: "Mr. Austin, isn't it a fact that you left the building, locked the door, and went home and went to bed?"

AUSTIN: "No. sir."

SMITH: "Mr. Austin, isn't it a fact that you actually did leave the dorm about 10 pm?"

AUSTIN: "No. Sir."

SMITH: "How can you explain, Mr. Austin [that] people who were not on duty, in bed, sound asleep, could located [sic] the fire before you did?"

AUSTIN: "I just don't know."[13]

With this last question and Austin's answer, there was no way to back out of it. Though Mrs. Austin had previously testified that her husband had not been home that night until the moment they were given news of the fire, she apparently was believed by no one.

Finally, Gaines was called by Smith, but unaccountably he was not asked to explain the contradictions that ran all through the statements he and Hall had given to reporters. Smith didn't follow through with these important questions even though Gaines might well have brushed them aside. Instead, Gaines was given questions that allowed him to establish that though he had assigned Austin and Hall to duties at the dorm, he didn't know whether Austin had been in the building or not. Smith did ask Gaines if he had questioned Austin and Hall after the fire, but Gaines claimed he had not. This response was curious, but Gaines explained it by saying, "I knew my Board would make a thorough investigation of this; I felt that I should leave it up to them, and not try to create prejudice on the part of any employee. I have refrained from discussing this with all of my staff as I want the facts derived from this investigation."[14]

Asked specifically if, at the time of the fire, he was asleep at the Superintendent's home," Gaines said he was: "The hospital called the Givan[s]" and "her husband got me out of bed." He did not mention and neither was he asked if he had spoken to Mrs. Givan on the telephone and instructed her to call the fire department. Nor did he mention that several boys had run to his house after escaping through the windows as reported in the press. Gaines told the board that the superintendent's house, located at the south end of the campus, was two and a half blocks from the big boys' dormitory and that when he arrived at the scene it was about ten after four in the morning. When he arrived, Fleming and Hall were already there trying to tear off windows. They were joined by Mattison later.

Smith asked Gaines about his instructions to the employees who served as night supervisors in the dorm that burned. Gaines replied he told them to stay in the building until the boys were checked the next morning. Asked who was assigned on March 4 to the "big boys" dorm, Gaines said, "Hall and Austin. Hall checking on Austin." And that had been the arrangement since February 21, when Banks went into the hospital. Asked what he meant by "Hall checking on Austin," Gaines said that since they had been working all day, they might fall asleep. "You might say it was just an added precaution—to insure that the boys were safe at all times."

Gaines was not content to remain on the defensive. When Smith asked him if there had been "any hazardous condition reported to him in connection with the dorm," Gaines said that in the last six months there had been. "*Bad wiring in the caretaker's room; and the floors are bad*" (emphasis added). Evidence that the fire may have started in the caretaker's room was significant information and a potential bombshell after Gaines said that he "*did not have sufficient funds [to have the entire building rewired]. . . . The necessary funds have to be appropriated by the Legislative Council*" (emphasis added). He added that he had appeared before the Legislative Council with information about the wiring.

With this statement, Gaines shifted part of the blame for the boys' deaths to the backs of the Arkansas legislature and to the governor himself, since it was highly unlikely that Gaines had made a request for funds without approval from the governor's office. Smith asked, "Can this statement be substantiated?" Gaines did not hesitate: "*Yes, I have copies of the report presented to the council*"[15] (emphasis added).

Minutes of a legislative subcommittee dated November 18, 1958, confirm that "Mr. Gaines presented a budget for major repairs to existing buildings and living quarters in the amount of $17,000....He pointed out that the dormitories . . . were all badly run down, and the additional request for repairs was badly needed."[16]

But Gaines was not through. Smith asked him, "Mr. Gaines, if these two employees [Hall and Austin] had functioned properly, would this tragedy have occurred?" Gaines answered, "There was no way they could have prevented the fire." In response to another question, Gaines said he would have taken steps to discipline and/or terminate the men had he known they were not doing their job, and after saying again he had not talked to anyone on the board or his staff about the hearing, Gaines was finished. Gaines, of course, had not answered the question that was, in fact, whether his employees could have prevented the deaths of the boys. Without information about where and what time the fire began, any truthful answer would have been only speculation.

The recommendation of the committee was signed by all three members of the board and read, "Based upon the facts brought out at this investigation, this Board is of the unanimous opinion that this tragedy could not have been prevented, that everyone concerned had attempted to carry his duty, and the persons directly charged with the supervision of the building in question, be severely reprimanded."

In retrospect, there are obviously a number of questions about the hearing beyond the puzzle of whether there were other witnesses. The most serious ones have to do with the failure of Alfred Smith to confront Gaines and Wilson Hall Jr. with all the contradictions in their stories, beginning with the superintendent's admission to the press that he hadn't thought it "necessary to assign another adult to sleep in the dormitory at night." Why didn't Alfred Smith zero in on the fact that Lester Gaines and Wilson Hall Jr. had given multiple stories that changed each time they tried to explain who had been on duty? Why did Smith cross-examine Lee Austin so rigorously and not Wilson Hall and Gaines? Why would Mrs. Givan have both documents in her possession at the hearing unless she had been told to bring them? And why would Exhibit "B" include both "Supt. and Mrs. L.R. Gaines" as a "campus resident"? For the almost six years Gaines had been superintendent, he and his wife had maintained a residence in Little Rock. How often he spent the night in Little Rock is not clear. No employees said that Mary Gaines, who had a full-time job in Little Rock, was a resident on the Wrightsville campus. Dorothy Mattison, whom I interviewed and whose memory was quite clear, remembers seeing Mary Gaines only rarely.[17]

CHAPTER SEVEN

Us versus Them

[In the United States] education is a synonym for
indoctrination if you are white and subjugation if you are black.
—**James Baldwin,** *The Price of the Ticket: Collected Nonfiction 1948–1985*

Suddenly, Orval Faubus was incommunicado. Rolla Fitch, his executive secretary, was telling the press the governor was at the mansion "sick." After reading on March 10 the transcript of the interviews conducted by Alfred Smith, no doubt the governor felt a bit under the weather whether he was running a fever or not. The board had come up with conclusions and a recommendation that were totally at odds with what he had expected and wanted.

Alfred Smith had told the press early Monday afternoon on March 9 that the board had completed its investigation and would release the report at 5:30 p.m. "at the school." But instead of making the report public, later in the afternoon Smith pushed back the date of the report's release until the next day, saying the report had to go to the governor for his review before it was made available to the press. Thus, instead of being made available to the public, suddenly the report was for Faubus's eyes only. Reversing what he had said about releasing the report, Smith told reporters, "This has been a confidential investigation at the request of the governor. He should be given the benefit of reviewing it." Smith said the board "hoped to meet with the governor" the next day [Tuesday] when the report would "probably be released" to the public, but he didn't know because the governor still might be sick. The board planned to attend the March 10 funerals of the fourteen boys whose bodies had been burned too badly to allow identification if it didn't conflict with the meeting with the governor.

That Tuesday an estimated three hundred mourners were staring at fourteen coffins under a tent at Haven of Rest Cemetery in Little Rock as they listened to the Reverend Charles Walker read from the Bible when the scream of a woman standing at the gravesite shattered the calm of the service. "Oh Lord! My baby, my baby," she moaned.

With this cry, she ran toward the coffins under the tent and was immediately followed by other sobbing parents. Mothers crowded up to the caskets. An elderly woman clasped her hands and paced outside the tent. "Lord, I didn't have but one boy. He was only fourteen years old. Oh Lord! You done burned him up." As she laid a white lily on each casket, another woman wailed, "Give one to all the babies."

Standing by one of the caskets, a mother cried, "My son, I'm here. Your mama is here." She then fell to her knees. A reporter observed the behavior of Superintendent Gaines. "He sat motionless, staring at the coffins. An occasional sob jarred his body. . . . 'I wish it could have been me,' Gaines said with tears in his eyes. 'Those boys only wanted someone to love them, and God and I loved them all. Loved them something awful.'"[1]

In light of what had been written by the press in the previous seventy-two hours, a sympathetic observer might have wondered if these were not only the words of a man whispered in abject grief but also in agony because of the guilt he was experiencing. A cynic might have speculated that the superintendent spoke them aloud in an effort to shape the public perception of him as a state employee who had deeply cared about the boys and had tried to do the best he could with the resources available to him.

Though Rolla Fitch told reporters that the board had turned over the results of its investigation to "the governor's office" on March 10, he was vague about its contents. The press neither mentioned the board's attendance at the funeral nor did it report a meeting with the governor. In an *Arkansas Democrat* article on March 11, Fitch told the press that "he didn't know why the board hadn't released the report [to the public] but that he wouldn't make it available. 'It's up to the Board to do so,' he said." This comment was disingenuous at best. The governor was calling the shots, and Fitch knew it. There had been nothing in the press previously about the report being "confidential," but now suddenly it was.

For the next two weeks, the press waited. Reporters concentrated on the events unfolding at the state capitol. In an *Arkansas Gazette* article analyzing the just completed fifty-day session, that newspaper's reporter, Ernest Valachovic, marveled at the governor's control over the legislature so long as the issue was race: "Every legislator knew it. Politicians all, they paid full respect to the master of the art. Time and time again the remark came out, when segregation was the subject of legislation, 'They elected the man for this so let's go on with it.'"[2]

Meanwhile, the news of the deaths of twenty-one boys, as previously mentioned, generated a far greater response outside the state than from Arkansans themselves. Though *Arkansas Democrat* publisher K. August Engel, as stated, had attributed the conditions at the NBIS to "long neglect" and a last place finish in the political process, those who wrote the governor from out of state charged him and the state with behavior that went beyond conduct associated with simple negligence, however long-standing.

A telegram from the Greater King Solomon Baptist Church in Detroit began, "We hold you and the Jim Crow System of the South just as responsible for the burning of the Negro Children in Little Rock as if you had struck the match." A couple from Los Angeles, California, wrote Faubus on March 5 that "we cannot help but feel that you must bear the ultimate responsibility for the death of these young Americans. As the leading elected official of your state, your support of a policy of segregation and of second-class citizenship for the Negro people helped to create this holocaust."

Carmen Ruthling, an eighteen-year-old college student at Arizona State University, began, "How utterly shocked and horrified I was to read of the deaths of twenty-one boys in the March 5th fire." Two paragraphs later, she wrote,

> perhaps if you cared more for the people of whom you are supposed
> to be the leader, you would see to it that boys such as these are not
> kept for months and months in reform schools, especially when they
> have committed no crimes. . . . You would see to it that the children
> and youths of Arkansas get an education, instead of closing all schools
> for nearly a whole school year.[3]

From Kansas City, Missouri, on March 6, Charles Austin wrote, in part, "May God forgive you and awaken you to realities, it is all-but too obvious that you, Mr. Governor, and your Senate and Legislature [House of Representatives] have spent far too much time trying to disenfranchise citizens and to circumvent the United States Supreme Court." In a handwritten letter dated March 8, A. H. Hill from Bluefield, Virginia, wrote,

> Sir, I hope your measly heart is capable of feeling the sting of the
> race hate you as a leader of your gang started last fall. . . . How low
> can a people stoop? You take advantage of a race, of your congress-
> man [Brooks Hays] of all the decency that should belong to a man in
> office. Really, I can't see how you can look yourself in a mirror without
> feeling the shame you brought to your office, to your state, and to your
> race. Only a depraved person could be so disgrace himself and not
> cringe with shame.[4]

As mentioned previously, the governor never shared publicly his reaction to these letters so sharply critical of him and the state nor did he respond himself. However, he did take the trouble to reply at length to a letter written by a group of black ministers who were members of the Commission on Race Relations of the National

Baptist Convention, the largest and most influential contingent of black Baptists in the United States. Their deferential tone, to wit, "The undersigned are distressed at this report [newspaper accounts] and are writing to ask Your Honor the following questions concerning the tragedy," may have played a part in his willingness to respond to questions about how the fire could have killed so many children. In a letter dated April 28, 1959, Faubus wrote that "there had been no injuries to others" and "if someone had been on duty, the fire could have been prevented or extinguished, or the boys could have escaped, everyone of them, without so much as a burned finger."[5] He asserted once again that the failure of the superintendent to assign an individual to spend the night at the dormitory amounted to "criminal negligence."

One of the two letters the governor received from an in-state resident suggests the effect that Faubus's tactics was having on his Arkansas critics. Identifying herself as white, a female correspondent wrote, "For surely the blood of these poor little kids is on your hands. God will remember on judgement [sic] day. Jus' niggers, eh? I voted for you last fall—but never—never again." It is unsigned. And for good reason. By 1959 Arkansas was privately said by whites who differed with Faubus's racial policies to be a "police state."[6] Faubus biographer Roy Reed notes that after 1957, "Much of [Faubus's] political behavior during the next several years was a blend of coded white supremacy and McCarthyism."[7]

It seemed to matter little to most white Arkansans in the 1950s that as Numan Bartley, a leading scholar of the period, put it, "Racial segregation no longer possessed the intellectual respectability that had accompanied Social Darwinism, biological determinism, and justifications for imperialism. A new school of anthropology and a changed intellectual atmosphere made a mockery of white supremacy, while American pretensions to world leadership added the insult of hypocrisy."[8]

Academic research disputing old stereotypes involving alleged black inferiority may have "made a mockery of white supremacy" but didn't end it in Arkansas or the South in general. Fresh thinking about the endurance of white supremacy was irrelevant for the overwhelming number of white Arkansans who needed only to consult the books and journal articles written in this era in their home state to confirm their view of how race relations should be followed.

Indeed, in the decade and a half before the fire, three of the state's busiest writers were defining Arkansas race relations for readers both young and old. One year before the boys were incinerated at Wrightsville, Dr. Walter L. Brown, then a young history professor at the University of Arkansas at Fayetteville, published in 1958 what would later be noted as a "widely used" state-approved school textbook for elementary students titled, *Our Arkansas*.[9] In chapter two, titled, "The Coming of the White Man to Arkansas," Dr. Brown writes, "Indians lived in the land *we* call Arkansas hundreds of years before *our European ancestors* knew anything about America"[10] (emphases added). On the same page, he mentions that Indians were "weaker" than the whites and "were pushed out." Since "their customs" have long been forgotten, "the history of Arkansas can be said to be the story of the white man in *our* state" (emphasis added).

Undisputedly a winner's version of history, *Our Arkansas* summarizes race relations by stating, "In these and hundreds of other ways white Arkansans forced the Negro to accept, for the time being, a place lower than that of the white man in the political, business and social life of the state."[11] This blunt declaration of white supremacy was hardly a new phenomenon in the South or in the nation.[12] Following long practice, the material in *Our Arkansas* relating to race echoes traditional accounts of previous Arkansas and southern history textbooks before the civil rights era. Accompanying the routine facts about the state's formation and growth are the usual omissions and misconceptions that earlier Arkansas historians had repeatedly made about race from the days of slavery forward.[13] For example, *Our Arkansas* states, "Nearly all the Negro slaves remained loyal to their white masters,"[14] a false and enduring fiction very useful to those white Arkansans who romanticized slavery.

In fact, the opposite was true. Historian Carl Moneyhon of the University of Arkansas at Little Rock writes that with the domination of Union ships in Arkansas waters by 1862, blacks deserted the plantations "in droves" and "well-treated slaves left as quickly as others."[15] *Our Arkansas* does not mention that over five thousand black troops were raised in Arkansas and many fought bravely and well against their former owners.[16] Rather, it informs the reader that "a few of the Negro men joined General Steele's army and fought against the Confederates."[17]

Our Arkansas does not disclose that during slavery Arkansas whites whipped, beat, murdered, raped, and split up black families; it devotes thirteen pages to the Civil War in Arkansas and the bravery of whites and then gives a highly exaggerated and biased account of the misdeeds that occurred during the Reconstruction Era due to Republican so-called misrule. Thus, after the defeat of the South, Arkansas fell into the hands of the "Radicals," who "were as selfish and as dishonest a crew of men as ever lived." These were the "Carpetbaggers" and "Scalawags" who "won the Negroes to the Republican Party by telling them it had won the Civil War and had given them their freedom." Rather than described as a murderous terrorist organization, the Ku Klux Klan was said to be necessary to protect "against the unruly Negroes,"[18] who "since they knew very little about taking care of themselves . . . soon became a real problem to the townspeople and to the government."[19]

In its portrayal of state racial history after Reconstruction ended, *Our Arkansas* concludes, "The result was that Arkansas remained, as it had been before the Civil War, 'a white man's country.'" Black Arkansans were the Other.

Interestingly, *Our Arkansas* expresses great sympathy for Native Americans:

> Arkansans believed that the Indians were not making proper use of their lands. They felt that the Indians must go and their lands must be settled by whites if Arkansas was to prosper.

The Indians, however, had no other place to go. They had been forced by greedy whites living east of the Mississippi to trade their old lands for new lands in Arkansas. Now greedy whites of Arkansas Territory wanted their new lands. The Indians must have felt that there was no end to their struggle against the selfish whites.

The Cherokees and Choctaws were not wild savages. They were civilized Indians, fast adopting the ways of the white man. . . . They owned Negro slaves and had cultivated large cotton plantations before their removal from east of the Mississippi."[20]

In contrast *Our Arkansas* makes no moral judgment about Arkansas whites who were involved in the ownership and selling of slaves nor does it condemn the behavior of Arkansas whites who participated in the terrorist activities of the Ku Klux Klan. This stark acknowledgement of white supremacy explicitly reflected the reality that black Arkansans could continue to expect to be treated in a way commensurate with their "lower" status despite the "separate but equal" doctrine enunciated by the Supreme Court in *Plessey v Ferguson* in 1896. *Our Arkansas* instructed its young readers, "You are fortunate to be an Arkansan and to live in so pleasant a state."[21] The Arkansans to whom this statement was intended were obviously white.

Had *Our Arkansas* not been written by one of the state's most distinguished academic historians, it would be easier to dismiss the book as an unrepresentative textbook that somehow slipped through the cracks. On the contrary, Dr. Brown went on to a laudable career as a scholar and editor of the *Arkansas Historical Quarterly* for over thirty years and was an effective advocate for a more balanced approach to the state's racial history. A plaque hangs in Ole Main at the University of Arkansas at Fayetteville honoring his contributions to Arkansas history and celebrates the fact that under his leadership, the *Quarterly* published some of the earliest scholarship on "African-Americans and civil rights history."[22] The fact remains, however, that the publisher of *Our Arkansas* brought out two more editions (not reprints) in 1953 and 1969 but none of the material on race, the Civil War, and Reconstruction was withdrawn or revised, but for an update in a few statistics (education, names of governors, and a slight revision of the index), the three editions appear to be identical in content and content.[23]

In 1956 Margaret Smith Ross, editor of the *Pulaski County Historical Review*, wrote a lengthy article titled "Have *We* Neglected Negro History?"(emphasis added) and concluded that "if the Negroes feel that the writing of their history has not been assumed satisfactorily by the white people, then qualified Negroes should undertake the task." But "in the past year and a half," she writes, "only one Negro has done any research at the Arkansas History Commission, and two have telephoned requests for information."

Ross, who wrote a history column for the *Arkansas Gazette*, was prompted to respond after "an unidentified Negro spokesman told a *Gazette* reporter, 'We regret the necessity of making a special point of the deeds of Negroes. Historians should have recorded those deeds along with those of white persons who made history.'"

The impetus for this complaint was the participation by black schools in Little Rock in the "30th annual nationwide observance of Negro History Week." At Horace Mann High School, one of the primary activities that week, Ross noted, was to compile an "honor roll which cited various groups and individuals for their efforts in promotion of racial integration during 1955, and a 'condemnation list' of those who had attempted to deter the integration program or had uttered major or minor slurs against the Negro."

In fact, as national historian W. Fitzhugh Brundage would many years later document in *The Southern Past: A Clash of Race and Memory* (2005), the Arkansas History Commission "inevitably focused on sites hallowed by whites. . . . Black newspapers, institutional records, and private correspondence went uncollected."[24] Brundage would contend that the "void in the collections of the South impeded opportunities to understand the Southern racial order from any perspective other than its architects."

In less academic language, the Arkansas History Commission had heavily stacked the deck, and as long as white historians were dealing the cards, black Arkansans had little hope of being acknowledged as active participants in the major decisions affecting their own lives. In fact, whites in this era rarely, if ever, credited blacks with having made any contributions to history. Anticipating Brundage's conclusion by almost fifty years, Ross argued that Arkansas "historians pride themselves on their objectivity, and would never maliciously ignore any important aspect of history, regardless of their personal prejudices. . . . We cannot agree that Negro contributions to history that are worthy of mention have been denied their proper proportion of attention in general histories."[25]

It was understood that the persons who were making the decisions about what was worth attention in general histories of Arkansas were white. Historians of this era may have "pride[d] themselves on their objectivity," but their work, like that of all historians, was inevitably influenced by the white supremacist culture and mentality of the time. As Exhibit "A," the most popular general Arkansas history in this era was written by Arkansas's then most lauded writer, one-time Harvard student John Gould Fletcher, who had won the state's only Pulitzer Prize for poetry. In 1933 Fletcher, a member of the southern literary coterie known as the Agrarians, had written a letter to the *The Nation* in which he purported to speak for the South: "But we are determined, whether rightly or wrongly, to treat him [the Negro] as a race largely dependent upon us, and inferior to ours."[26]

Given his announced intentions, it follows that Fletcher's general history, titled *Arkansas*, first published in 1947 by the University of North Carolina Press and then reprinted in 1989 by the University of Arkansas Press, contains almost nothing about 25 percent of the state's population. His characterization of the southern slave owners and blacks in the antebellum period suggests the reason for this omission:

Slavery to them was of the natural order of things. The Negroes had never been anything else but slaves, and the institution always working well when the slaveowner behaved as every decent man should behave, needed no defenders, and found none till the abolitionists drew attention to its supposed injustices. What these Southerners really hated, and fought against, was not the Negroes but the Indians . . . they had learned the lesson, in the twenty years following the Revolution, that the Indians had to be exterminated. That five important tribes, at last, were still settled on good Southern land—guaranteed them by foolish treaties—was an outrage. From Jackson down to the half-savage frontiersman, the feeling ruled that they must go.[27]

Later Fletcher wrote, "We who are both civilized and aware of the failure of civilization to provide any solution for human want, misery and injustice, can afford to sympathize with the five civilized tribes who, in their great crisis, bore themselves nobly and shamed the lust of the land-greedy white men. The Arkansawyers of that day thought differently: they wasted but little sympathy."[28]

Before dismissing *Arkansas* as the work of a depressed suicide, the critic should be aware that Arkansas historian Dr. Ben F. Johnson III, in his biography of John Gould Fletcher, notes that though the quality of Fletcher's published work over his lifetime was extremely uneven (likely because of his chronic deep depressions), he gives high marks to the quality of the writing in *Arkansas*, stating that its "vivid dramatic action and elegant descriptions mark it as Fletcher's superior prose achievement."[29] Johnson writes that "African Americans figured but little in Fletcher's history. Slavery was offhandedly mentioned as an inevitable development of migration from other states, and black Arkansans during Reconstruction were portrayed as bewildered pawns of the feuding white factional leaders."

Completing *Arkansas* in 1947, Fletcher goes to great lengths to describe the pernicious sharecropper system that dominated much of the state's economy during his lifetime. According to Fletcher's informants, namely, Arkansas planters, blacks were naturally suited to the sharecropper system with their innate tolerance for the hur-ry-up and wait cycle of planting and harvesting a cotton crop, but the system somehow exploited whites who "are less adjusted to the periods of forced labor followed by spells of idleness."[30]

The above constitutes the sum total of Fletcher's analysis of Arkansas racial history from slavery to 1947. Though *Arkansas* received modestly respectful reviews from a variety of national sources including the *New York Times* for the vividness of its prose, the lack of meaningful analysis and insight into the state's racial problems made it of popular interest only to white Arkansans.

Not discussed by the three writers was Arkansas's actual racial history. An exception in this era is Orville Taylor's *Negro Slavery in Arkansas*, published in 1958 by the Duke University Press. As Professor Carl Moneyhon of the University of Arkansas at Little Rock explains in his introduction to the 2000 reprint of the book by the University of Arkansas Press, *Negro Slavery in Arkansas* was a major advance in the scholarly presentation of the slave era in Arkansas. Analytical and heavily sourced, Taylor's use of primary sources at the time became the gold standard for Arkansas historians.

Writing in 2000, Moneyhon calls the book "an important addi-tion to the revisionist literature of its time" and says that it "is the necessary starting point for any future study of slavery in Arkan-sas."[31] In fact, there had been no full-length book treatment of Arkansas slavery until Dr. Taylor's book, which was derived from his dissertation on the subject at Duke. Dr. Moneyhon traces the historiography of the subject and places *Negro Slavery in Arkansas* on the spectrum between those academic historians who had in lockstep followed the analysis of Ulrich Bonnell Phillips and those historians who had begun to call into question much of what Phil-lips had written, primarily challenging his view that slavery had not been profitable. Another point of difference was that Phillips looked kindly upon slaveowners.

What Taylor apparently did not do was research in any depth black primary sources in order to explore bondage from the point of view of the enslaved themselves and thus only told one side of the story.[32] For example, he appears not to have consulted the approximately 186 interviews of persons of African descent who experienced slavery in Arkansas. Conducted by the writers for the Works Progress Administration in the 1930s, these interviews and other primary materials provide a much more brutal picture of the institution but at the same time present formerly enslaved persons as self-directed individuals.[33]

It has only been relatively recently that Arkansas scholars writing about race have forthrightly taken on the unenviable but necessary task of directly challenging the work of earlier historians. Most instructive is Blake Wintory's reading of local efforts by earlier Arkansas historians. For example, Dr. Wintory points out that

> the DAR version of local history represented a *selective tradition* that intentionally emphasized certain meanings and interpretation of the past while excluding others as a means to *justify* the present. The selective tradition of "Lost Cause" narratives cast African-American political struggles as the disingenuous product of an inferior group manipulated by corrupt northern carpetbaggers.[34] (emphases added)

One might also conclude that it was not merely "local" historians who represented a "selective tradition" in writing about Arkansas and race. Others did as well.

CHAPTER EIGHT

Hanging Together

I don't care what they say. . . . They let 21 boys
burn up and it could have been prevented.
—**Orval Faubus,** *Arkansas Gazette*, March 26, 1959

On March 25, following his usual practice of holding a press conference at a time when the *Arkansas Gazette* could not scoop the
Arkansas Democrat, the governor called state capitol beat reporters
together and announced, "I am recommending to the board that
L. R. Gaines be discharged immediately. I am recommending also
the discharge of Mrs. Gaines, B. T. Humphrey [sic] and Wilson Hall,
Jr." Further, he was recommending that all employees be put on
"probation when a new superintendent was hired."

According to the governor, an attempt at a cover-up by Gaines
had come apart when employees Wilson Hall and Lee Austin had
been escorted by a "colored friend" of his to the governor's mansion
for a Sunday night visit so they could talk to him privately. Hall
and Austin told him that Gaines had pressured them into making
statements that were false. The governor said, "The investigation
showed . . . that Gaines got employees together after the fire and
coached them in a story to tell investigators. . . . They also told me
that ever since the other employe[e] had been in the hospital . . .
that they locked the boys up about 7 or 8 at night and then went
home." Investigations by the State Police and the fire marshal had
"not determine[d] the cause of the fire, but the agencies did find
that the youths had been locked inside the dormitory and no one

was near with a key to release them when the fire started." According to the governor, there was no evidence of arson. He said he would be providing the Wrightsville board "all the papers on the investigation by various state agencies." Despite these comments, Faubus acknowledged at the press conference that "there was some evidence of frayed electric wires also which could have contributed to the fire."[1] This admission was highly significant, but as on the day of the fire, not a single reporter asked the obvious questions: "Could have *contributed* to the fire?" Governor, haven't you just admitted the fire marshal found evidence of the possible *cause* of the fire? Why won't you make public the fire marshal's report? Why won't you make public the State Police investigation? Why won't you make public the Board's investigation? Why have you refused to release the minutes of past board meetings? Why didn't you appoint board members to replace those whose terms had expired? Why didn't you do something about the dormitory? Why have you refused to respond to requests from the board and the superintendent to provide a new dormitory and basic maintenance of the infrastructure at Wrightsville?

Had reporters been given access to the past minutes, these documents would have revealed how systematically unresponsive the governor was to the conditions at Wrightsville. As mentioned, from long practice Faubus was a master at making allegations that weren't supported by facts or at best were half-truths. Besides, Wrightsville was an easy target. He didn't have to say in his initial press conference why he had said that all the employees were "Negroes." It was a thinly veiled way of saying that, well, what could you expect from a black institution?

At the same time, during this period Faubus displayed what appeared to be genuine concern for the plight of parents who had children at Wrightsville. In a response to a letter from a parent worried that she had not heard from her son after the fire, the governor assured her that he had called Wrightsville on her behalf: "Goldie is perfectly all right. I can't imagine why he hasn't written to keep you from worrying but the school officials assured me that they would ask him to write a letter in a few days."[2]

More than fifty years later, Hot Springs survivor James Watson independently confirmed the concern over the condition of the wiring expressed by Lester Gaines when questioned by Alfred Smith. In a recorded, thirty-four-page interview supplemented by written questions and answers, Watson, eighteen at the time of the fire, volunteered the following:

> Q. You mentioned that the wiring had no insulation, and you also mentioned a "loft." Was the loft a space in or above the ceiling? How did you know the wire had no insulation?
> A. Yes, the loft was a space above the ceiling. Because the power used to go off for three or four hours at a time, "Scrapiron" and I pushed up the cover of the loft one day to try to figure out the reason and that's when we saw all the naked wiring. There were [sic] no insulation whatsoever. I can't remember Scrapiron [sic] real name. That was his nickname. We called everybody by their nicknames. I think he was the one burned in the fire.[3]

The governor then told reporters that after learning of the pressure exerted by the superintendent, he had "broadened" the investigation to take a look at the payroll and found "M. P. Gaines" was being compensated. A year earlier he had been informed that Mary Gaines was a full-time teacher at Dunbar Junior High in Little Rock. He had told the superintendent to get his wife off the payroll (she was receiving $115 monthly), and Gaines had "sat right here in this office and promised" he would do so. In addition, he had discovered that a man by the name of B. T. Pumphrey was receiving a check as well.

The governor said he had asked around and neither board members nor staff "mentioned ever seeing him around the school." When asked what Pumphrey did to earn $140 monthly, Gaines had told him that he repaired televisions. Faubus told the media that "he knew of only two television sets at the school." Though not mentioned in the article and perhaps unknown to the governor at that time, Pumphrey was the brother of Mary Gaines.[4]

The afternoon after the story appeared in the *Democrat*, the superintendent and his wife, as well as a majority of the staff at Wrightsville, took the unprecedented step of publicly confronting the governor. Eleven of the nineteen employees hurriedly put together an individually signed statement of support for Buddy and Mary Gaines, calling the governor's allegation that they had been pressured to make a false statement "an insult to our integrity." The employees "implied they might resign if they are placed on probation as the governor had suggested."[5]

Though summarized in the *Arkansas Gazette* on March 26, the full statement by the employees would be carried only in the weekly *State Press* on April 3. The *State Press* article pointed out that the same conditions still existed at Wrightsville as had existed when Faubus had made a visit to the school "a little over a year ago" and found 'inexcusable' conditions which were so 'deplorable.'" The statement then posed the questions that no one else in Arkansas had addressed publicly:

> Did Mr. Faubus recommend then that finance [sic] be appropriated to correct any of these "deplorable" conditions? ... Why has he not published the actual cause of the fire instead of engaging in the character assassination of the Superintendent and members of the staff [?] Why should we be blamed for something that others have stated could happen at many other state agencies?

The eleven employees "agreed with the Governor that the fire was 'inexcusable' but not due to the negligence on the part of the Superintendent, Mr. R. L. [sic] Gaines, or any employee of the school." Addressing the governor, the board, and the public, the statement read, "We know Mr. Gaines to be conscientiously dedicated to the well being of each delinquent and neglected boy committed to his care, and to the improvement of the institution as a whole with the limited facilities permitted him. . . . A respectable man, with his sterling character and long unblemished public record would not belittle himself to use cheap pressure tactics." Knowing they had to deal with the allegations of the governor that Austin and Hall had come to the governor's mansion, the eleven included in their statement the following: "A sworn notarized statement from one of us, whose name was mentioned by Mr. Faubus as having given him a 'corrected version' of our testimony, is available stating that he did not see Mr. Faubus or any of his representatives at the mansion or any other place." Though never identified by the media, this individual was surely Wilson Hall Jr., since he was the individual Faubus recommended firing. Mary Gaines, also, was mentioned in the statement, which said "we also know how closely Mrs. Gaines works with him in his efforts." In the *State Press* article accompanying the statement, L. C. Bates wrote, "Mrs. Gaines works at the school after hours, holidays, Saturdays and Sundays." The article mentions that the governor claimed he had told Gaines to take his wife off the payroll.

For his part, Gaines said he was not going to resign and would discuss the matter with his board. He claimed he didn't comprehend why the governor was singling out employees. "The "Board gave me discretion to hire," Gaines stated. He said "his wife and the others were employed at the school with the knowledge of the board." Echoing her husband, that night Mary Gaines issued a statement in which she said the decision to put her on the payroll was not hers "but an agreement with the board to supplement my husband's low salary. . . . The Board was shrewd enough to know that they were going to get a lot of work done for a little money. When we came into this situation only a humanitarian or a complete fool would have remained, due to the deplorable conditions that we found at the school." Mrs. Gaines wasn't through. She added, "Because I am a public servant [a public school teacher in Little Rock], I have felt before certain political pressures but not once did I believe that they would come from the chief executive of the state."

Unasked by the press was also the question of why the governor had not also recommended firing Lee Austin, for he, too, had given "unreliable information." In his press conference on March 25, Faubus had said the "story included something about the guard leaving the building to get a flashlight." As noted, it was Lee Austin who had given this account, but Faubus did not mention him by name. For not changing his story, as apparently Wilson Hall Jr. had done by signing an affidavit to the effect that he had not talked with Faubus, Austin would get to keep his job at least through this period. Neither Austin's nor his wife's name appear on the statement by the Wrightsville employees.

Upon learning of the employees' response, Faubus was furious. "I don't care what they say," he shot back. "I'm going to straighten it [the school] out. They let 21 boys burn up and it could have been prevented."[6]

In fact, the governor was already looking for Lester Gaines's replacement. On letterhead stationary dated March 24 from the Conway County sheriff's office in Morrilton, a day before the press conference, Sheriff Marlin Hawkins, one of the most infamous political operatives in the state, and two others (Loid Sadler and Rufus Morgan) wrote a letter of recommendation for "our good friend, Rupert E. Hemphill, who has made application for the position of Superintendent of the Negro Boys Industrial School at Wrightsville."

Sheriff Hawkins reminded the governor of Rupert Hemphill's steadfastness in the service of the Arkansas Democratic Party: "We have called on Rupert at midnight and at noon, and he has never failed to respond and to do the things that we have requested of him." He reminded the governor of the times "in the many years of your administration" when he and Sadler and Morgan "had bragged on several of our colored friends as being staunch members of the Democratic Party, and [these friends] have always been loyal to us to and your administration."

Speaking for the three of them, Sheriff Hawkins wrote, "We take great pleasure in recommending Rupert to you, and knowing that he will always be loyal to you and your administration." As for his qualifications to be superintendent, Hawkins noted that "Rupert has two years in college, and his wife has 3 years, and they are highly intelligent people, industrious, sober and loyal."[7]

The next day, on March 27 in an editorial titled, "School Head Should be Fired," *Arkansas Democrat* publisher K. August Engel gave his response to the governor's press conference. "There can be no question that Governor Faubus is right in recommending that L.R. Gaines be discharged."

It made no difference to Engel whether or not "the superintendent's version of the night watch is correct," because in Engel's view there were other compelling reasons to fire Gaines. He listed Gaines's decision to keep his wife on the payroll and the hiring of B. T. Pumphrey to keep the televisions in working order. Keeping "a few televisions in shape at the school . . . would still be an inexcusable expenditure in an institution that has needed essential things throughout its existence."

The *Arkansas Gazette* took no editorial position concerning the merits of the governor's investigation; however, opposing Orval Faubus in the aftermath of the fire in 1959 was his most persistent black critic, an African American man that historians, both black and white, have largely forgotten. Outside of Arkansas, some may remember Daisy Bates, but her husband, L. C. Bates, probably not at all. Though in December 1957 the Associated Press had selected Daisy Bates as its Woman of the Year in Education for her civil rights advocacy during the Central High School desegregation crisis, by 1959 she was spending more time outside of Arkansas than in it.

L. C. Bates, on the other hand, continued to publish the weekly *State Press*. From its first issue in 1941 until he and Daisy Bates were forced to close it in the fall of 1959, the paper was a hard-hitting civil rights tabloid modeled on the *Chicago Defender* and the NAACP's *The Crisis*. From the beginning, Bates was running inch-high headlines that, for example, roared, "CITY PATROL-MAN SHOOTS NEGRO SOLDIER, BODY RIDDLED WHILE LYING ON GROUND, WHITE MILITARY POLICE LOOK ON." In March 1942, on the front page of the *State Press*, he wrote the shooting was one of the "most bestial murders in the annals of Little Rock tragedies."[8]

Much more than just the supportive husband of his famous wife Daisy Bates, L. C. Bates was said by some contemporaries to be the "brains behind the operation." As an editor, he was persistently critical of his own people in the pages of the *State Press*. On more than one occasion, he said that between a principle and a friend, he would sacrifice the friend, and L. C. Bates was a man who meant it. How many newspapers ran a weekly cartoon as did the *State Press* captioned, "Do's and Don't's" that instructed African Americans to avoid boorish, offensive behavior in public? A typical cartoon read, "Don't Spit on the Street" or "Don't clown in Public."

For a time he even ran a column called "Mornin' Jedge" that recited reported arrests of Little Rock blacks culled from the police blotter. Critical of local black preachers whom he felt routinely sold out their congregations to white politicians for a few dollars, Bates was once successfully sued for libel. Interviewed in 1972, he would tell a reporter for the *Arkansas Gazette*, "The average Negro, you see, instead of trying to improve himself, is standing around begging and complaining. I have never been one to seek popularity. I'd rather be what I term right any time. That's the way it is with me."[9]

Today, these words are still jarring in the extreme, so politically incorrect they are almost laughable. It was not as if L. C. Bates delivered these sentiments from some lofty perch far from the black masses. From day one, the *State Press* had its offices in Little Rock on Ninth Street, the heart and soul of the black community.

But right or wrong, L. C. Bates had arguably earned the right to say what he thought. For criticizing white police brutality and Jim Crow laws and insisting on equal rights and opportunities for

Arkansas blacks over three decades, the home of L. C. and Daisy Bates had been firebombed and crosses had been burned in their yard seven times. Their once-profitable newspaper had been destroyed through a successful boycott by white advertisers and intimidation of distributors. Employed in 1960 as the field representative for the national office of the NAACP in Arkansas, L. C. Bates was so out of step with the tactics and strategies of the modern civil rights movement that the Arkansas NAACP hierarchy would eventually convince the national office to retire him.

On April 3, L. C. Bates blasted Orval Faubus in the lead editorial in the weekly *State Press* with the caption, "Is Governor Faubus Using NBIS Personnel For One of His Escape Holes?" After describing the deaths of the twenty-one boys, Bates bluntly accused the governor of Arkansas of "attempting to cover up the state's discrimination . . . by taking the investigation made by his office and laying the blame entirely upon the shoulders of the school's personnel, and even recommends a wholesale firing of employees."

Not only did Bates call the governor a liar, he added that he lied every time he opened his mouth: "Those of us who know the governor's tactics, cannot take too seriously any statement that the governor makes. His blame on the personnel of the school for the tragic happenings, could easily be one of the 'holes' that the governor boasts about to make his escape when trapping appears evident."

Though in the past the Little Rock power structure had taken the *State Press* seriously enough to offer L. C. Bates a bribe to soften the paper's message that he refused to accept,[10] the paper was now running on fumes. Now down to two thousand readers from a high of twenty thousand, the paper was on its last leg. It would go out fighting.

◆ ◆ ◆

After a tour of the campus by the Wrightsville board the morning of April 1, 1959, Alfred Smith promptly at 10 a.m. called to order the monthly meeting of the Wrightsville official overseers of the school. Two new board members, Ralph Van Meter from Judsonia and Fred W. Martin from Hot Springs, were seated "in accordance with the policies of the board." The board took up unfinished business. Superintendent Gaines gave his report as if nothing out of the ordinary were about to occur in the next twenty-four hours, stating that "all grounds were being prepared for planting." He said that "no action had been taken on the planting agreement with Mr. Buddy Hackett of Hackett's Seed Store, Little Rock, which was discussed at the previous meeting."[11] A phone call to Buddy Hackett during the meeting revealed that he had made other arrangements for the coming season.

As it did every month, the board considered those individuals up for parole. Gaines announced the present "enrollment" as "97" and said the school was "terribly crowded," as the "larger boys are domiciled in a converted classroom in the same building" with the smaller boys. The Mattisons were living in the building as well, and "Mr. Fleming relieves Mr. Mattison as supervisor in addition to having four night sergeants who patrolled the building constantly. Asked if all persons concerned had access to keys to the building, Mr. Gaines said they did."

J. C. Hawkins was elected as vice chairman of the board by acclamation; A. E. Woods was elected secretary and Fred Martin chaplain. Other matters were considered. The superintendent said that "a tool shed was to be constructed of concrete blocks and this building would also serve as a Trade Shop. He stated that the foundation has already been laid for the building." Chairman Alfred Smith noted, without apparent irony, "It was a pleasure to work with a full Board for the first time."[12]

Whether Gaines held out any hope that Alfred Smith would go to bat for him seems unlikely. Given the history of Wrightsville and the fact that governors in the past routinely got rid of board members whose decisions they didn't like would suggest it was not a fight worth making even if Smith had wanted to. Whether it was true that Smith or any others on the board had known that Mary Gaines and/or her brother were on the payroll, as both Gaines and his wife claimed, is not known.

In any event, after a discussion "in its entirety" of the investigation by the board and the State Police relative to the fire, J. C. Hawkins moved "that the services of the Superintendent Mr. L.R. Gaines, his wife, Mrs. M. P. Gaines, Mr. B.T. Pumphrey and Mr. Wilson Hall be terminated." While the vote was not recorded in the minutes, his motion was seconded and apparently approved.

The board also apparently followed the governor's recommendation concerning the other employees. The minutes state that the board "concluded that no further action be taken until a new superintendent is hired and that he be given the benefit of making a full and careful investigation of his own and report his findings to the Board at its next regular meeting."

Buddy Gaines asked to be allowed into the meeting "to address the Board, whereupon he tendered his resignation, which read as follows: 'I am this day submitting my resignation as Superintendent. . . . I feel it will be in the best interest of all concerned.'" After he was excused, J. C. Hawkins again moved that the board accept the resignation of Lester and Mary Gaines, whose letter of resignation was given to the board. Again no vote was recorded in the minutes, and the motion may not have carried. Eleven employees then asked and were permitted to address the board. In an act of solidarity with their superintendent, they, too, submitted a signed letter of resignation which read as follows:

We wish to express our appreciation to the Board and to Mr. Gaines for the pleasant association during the time that we have worked at the school. Due to the fact that our Superintendent's services are being terminated and our employment probationary, we offer this resignation to be effective on the date of Mr. Gaines's departure.

Again, J. C. Hawkins moved that this letter of resignation be accepted, and his motion was apparently approved unanimously. The board then interrupted its regular business to hold a press conference. Chairman Smith announced to newsmen the firing of four employees, including Lester and Mary Gaines. Though Gaines "told newsmen that he submitted his resignation," Smith made no mention of Gaines's "resignation" when announcing the termination. He told newsmen that Gaines was fired "because of negligence in connection with the school fire." He said that Wilson Hall Jr. was being terminated "because he had given 'unreliable information' in an investigation of the tragedy." Mary Gaines, Smith said, "was carried on the payroll even though she had another full-time job," and B. T. Pumphrey was fired because he "did little work at the institution." The *Democrat* reported that after reading a "formal statement about the dismissals," Chairman Smith revealed the resignation of eleven employees "who previously had made it clear they thought Gaines was being persecuted in the investigation." The employees, whose names weren't given to the press, were presumably those who had signed the statement supporting Gaines. Smith acknowledged that "only three old staff members remain but those resigning will stay at the school until successors are hired."[13]

Faubus had gotten his way as had every governor before him, but the board still had an institution to run. Though the events in the last month would be interpreted to suggest Lester Gaines was a hapless administrator of a dysfunctional institution, the extraordinary show of support by most of the employees at the NBIS indicated a picture much different from the one painted by the governor.

Though Gaines had been fired by the Wrightsville board the day before, he was still controlling events at the school as late as the night of April 3. At that time, a call came in to the State Police Criminal Investigation Division (CID) from "J.C. Hawkins, a Member of the Negro Boys Industrial School Board." Jeffrey Hawkins needed advice and needed it quick. He told a CID employee that

Superintendent Rupert Hemphill had called him and "asked if he could get a State Policeman to circle the area down there."[14]

The governor obviously had thought that Rupert Hemphill would hit the ground running. Hemphill had taken possession of the superintendent's house, but already his wife and children were frightened. Hemphill told Hawkins that "the boys were very restless and . . . twenty [20] of the boys had left the premises the previous night. He advised Hawkins that his family was afraid and that they wouldn't sleep any that night. Hawkins wanted to know what to do about it."

After numerous phone calls to superiors, the CID sent a captain and three other officers to the new superintendent's home, where they "found Hemphill's family upset." A quick count revealed twelve boys missing, "six of whom were runaways and six of whom were out on weekend passes." Jeffrey Hawkins and Alfred Smith pulled into the school shortly thereafter. In two reports marked "Confidential File," CID personnel wrote,

> Mr. Smith advised those present that there was not a thing to worry about and that he thought Mr. Hemphill could very well take care of the situation. In fact, he stated that he could see no reason for the State Police being called. Mr. Smith turned to Captain Templeton and stated, "Don't you think that everything is alright [sic]"? Captain Templeton stated to Mr. Smith, "No, I don't know that everything is alright [sic], but if you feel that you do not need our assistance we will go."

Board chairman Smith was surely imagining another story about the Wrightsville institution in the next day's papers. Ever since the board had exonerated Gaines with its report, the governor had taken matters into his own hands. He would not want to see or hear another word about him in connection with the institution.

Following up "with additional information" in a separate report, the officers noted:

There were no adults on the premises except Hemphill, the Superintendent, and Lee Andrew Auston [sic] who was working in someone
else's place. Hemphill told Mr. Hawkins that Mr. Gaines told him
that the other employees hadn't had a weekend off in (five) (5) weeks
and he was going to let them off for the weekend, and Mr. Hawkins
informed Hemphill at the time that as of the day he was hired, that
he was the Boss and was in full charge and was responsible and that
Gaines had no authority to give anyone the weekend off.[15]

How many boys came back that night or what happened to them
is not recorded.

With this rocky beginning, the leadership of the Negro Boys
Industrial School changed hands. If it was true that Buddy Gaines
had given the employees this particular weekend off, his behavior
seems the height of irresponsibility, but without more information it is impossible to judge what was occurring at that particular
moment.

If the former superintendent and his wife thought they could
get on with their lives, they were badly mistaken. Almost as soon
as Gaines was out as superintendent, the Legislative Joint Auditing Committee began an investigation of the finances at Wrightsville. Reporting to the governor on April 17, it purported to confirm
what Faubus had alleged in his press conference. In the words of
the *Arkansas Democrat*, the committee's report "was loaded with
accounts of questionable practices of former Supt. L.R. Gaines." One
of the major findings of the audit was that "warrants were made
out to Gaines's brother-in-law, B.T. Pumphrey, during a time when
the latter lived in Chicago." Claiming that Pumphrey did plumbing and radio repair at the school in addition to fixing televisions,
Gaines told auditors that Pumphrey had donated his salary in the
form of a $500 US Savings Bond to be given to the boys when they
left the institution. An auditor could confirm only three trips by
Pumphrey to Wrightsville and noted that the savings bond mentioned by Gaines was dated March 24. The press did not report how

long Pumphrey received a paycheck. Other irregularities included "a variety of handwriting styles used to endorse warrants made payable to several employees at the institution and on which Gaines was the secondary endorser." Though Gaines explained that he sometimes cashed warrants for employees, the obvious implication of the legislative audit report was that he had been forging their signatures. The special audit also noted that in 1955, the regular audit had revealed that Mrs. Gaines was on the Wrightsville payroll at the same time she was employed full-time at Dunbar Junior and Senior High School.

Almost as an afterthought, "another item questioned in the report was the lease of 2,095 acres of farm and pasture lands to Dr. T. J. Raney, Little Rock, for $4,692. Lawrence [County] Rep. Paul Graham said this figure sounds pretty low." But apparently this matter was getting too close for comfort, since Raney, as mentioned earlier, was a close personal friend and supporter of the governor. According to the article, the committee discussed whether it, as a body, had the authority to recommend criminal prosecution but decided discretion was the better part of valor and sent the audit over to the governor to allow him to make the decision of what to refer to the prosecuting attorney.[16] It would not be the last time questions would be raised about Dr. Raney's involvement with the farm.

On April 30, the governor sent Dr. Louis Coggs "a belated reply" in which he stated that "arrangements set by the Board of Control [the Wrightsville Board], with my knowledge and approval provided for at least one adult . . . to remain on duty in the building with the boys after they retired for the night." That had not occurred on March 7. After the governor explained that the regular person on duty was ill, "Superintendent Gaines then neglected to assign and keep someone on duty in the building with the boys. . . . The boys were locked in the building at night, then all the personnel went away to their homes, or to places off the premises of the school, leaving the boys completely unattended. . . . To my mind, this is criminal negligence, and should be punished accordingly." The governor claimed that "had someone been on duty, as they should have been, the fire could have been prevented or extinguished, or the boys could have escaped, everyone [sic] of them, without so much as a burned finger."

As mentioned previously, the statement of this author was only a guess, but the governor continued, stating that he had turned over the reports of the investigation "to an attorney in my office, who has presented it to the Prosecuting Attorney" to determine if charges should be filed against "Superintendent Gaines and any others."[17]

Now no longer employed and in disgrace, Buddy Gaines was said to be a changed man. Though a generation younger, African American attorney Christopher Mercer, who for a few months had served as field representative for the NAACP and advised Daisy Bates during the Little Rock Crisis, had known Buddy and Mary Gaines for around "15 to 20 years" before the fire. Though acknowledging that they had not been close friends, he said, "I recall that Mr. Gaines had always been held in high esteem in his role at the institution before this incident. He was always an outgoing person, with a contagious personality. After this incident he became a recluse, and he very seldom was seen in public. He eventually left town and I never saw him again."[18]

Mary Gaines was still employed by the Little Rock School District at Dunbar Junior High until school was out in the spring, but in light of the publicity surrounding Wrightsville, she would have known that like her husband, she probably had no future in the Little Rock public schools. Lester Gaines would have had little to do except wonder whether he was going to be criminally indicted. One assumes it was during this period they began to consider leaving the state as so many blacks had before them.

Meanwhile, families of the deceased boys had begun filing claims in March, right after the fire, for damages through the Arkansas Claims Commission. Arkansas law, like other jurisdictions, provides an administrative procedure for individuals who have been harmed by actions attributable to the state to seek compensation through an administrative process. Because of English common law and legal precedents long in place ("the King can do no wrong"), state legislatures enacted laws to allow citizens to circumvent the formal judicial system by creating the fiction that this particular administrative process does not constitute a lawsuit against the state. In all other respects, this legislative creature looked and acted like a lawsuit, with lawyers and legal arguments and hearings before a commission that mostly followed legal procedures.

The hearings for the boys who died in the fire took place on June 22 and 23.[19] More than fifty years after the fire, among their other grievances, Luvenia Long and her son Frank Lawrence still have trouble understanding why and how their family ended up with so little compensation after the lawyers got through with their business. The answer does not bring honor on the legal profession. Before a probate court ordered a final distribution of Lindsey's estate in 1961, three different Pulaski County law firms would be involved, purportedly on the estate's behalf. It cannot be established at this date who was most directly responsible, but the result for the heirs of Lindsey Cross would be a travesty of justice.

Though it is possible for one to go through the Claims Commission process without counsel, licensed attorneys routinely (as is common in civil personal injury law cases) represent claimants without charge in return for a percentage of the recovery. In order to receive compensation, claimants must show that the act or failure to act was the proximate cause of the harm, the same standard used in civil cases brought in a court of law. As in civil law cases, the Claims Commission statutes permit certain family members to seek compensation for the wrongful death of an individual caused by the state.

To facilitate the matter, the attorneys for the twenty claimants (administrators of the boys' estates) and two attorneys for the state of Arkansas agreed and stipulated that "all the testimony introduced to establish and prove negligence on the part of the officers, agents and employees of the State of Arkansas in the hearing of one certain claim should extend to and be the same testimony in all the other claims." This routine agreement served the claimants' interest since all the boys who died were in the same dormitory. Apparently overlooked in this proceeding were boys who had been burned in the fire but had escaped. Who they were and the extent of their injuries was not recorded.

The claimant chosen to represent the other nineteen who filed claims was that of "Willie Piggee, Administrator of the Estate of William Loyd Piggee, Deceased."[20] The law firm of McMath Leatherman and Woods represented the claimant Willie Piggee but also had been retained as the attorney for six other estates (including the estate of Lindsey Cross) of the deceased boys. With its reputation as a group of lawyers that supported black aspirations, this law firm of former governor Sidney McMath was an obvious choice.

Also listed as an attorney for the estate of Lindsey Cross with the McMath firm was a lawyer named Carl Langston. In addition to these two firms, attorney W. J. Walker was appointed by Pulaski County probate judge Guy Williams as administrator of the Lindsey Cross Estate. Why the mother of Lindsey Cross was not named as administrator of her son's estate is a mystery, since she had raised Lindsey all his life and was living in Pulaski County. Her former husband, Charlie Cross, was a resident of Detroit at the time of the appointment of W. J. Walker and had been gone from Little Rock for years.

As the reason for seeking to have himself serve as the administrator of Lindsey's estate, petitioner W. J. Walker, a Little Rock attorney, states merely, "The father, Charlie Cross has requested petitioner to serve as Administrator." There is nothing in the Lindsey Cross probate court file other than the word of W. J. Walker, which demonstrates that Charlie Cross had made this request. The order appointing Walker as administrator states that "the court, after hearing the petition and oral testimony in support thereof, and being well and sufficiently advised as to all of the facts in the premises, doth find that Lindsey Cross died March 5, 1959 in Little

Rock, Arkansas and that the court doth grant the prayer of the petitioner."[21]

Though inaccurate in two respects (Lindsey Cross died at the Negro Boys Industrial School and his mother did not go by the name of "Cross"), this language was routine boilerplate; still, it raises questions about the proceeding. The probate court file at the Pulaski County Courthouse contains no documents indicating that Lindsey's mother was given notice of the proceeding, nor does it contain a waiver of notice of the hearing signed by her.

Had the probate judge examined the petition and file, he would have immediately questioned why she had not been given notice of the proceeding. The petition for the appointment of an administrator inexplicably states that Charlie Cross (father) and Luvenia Cross [sic] (mother) were Lindsey's only "surviving heirs at law." Had anyone consulted Luvenia, she would have reported that Lindsey had three half siblings, and any knowledgeable attorney would have known that being a half sibling was not a bar to recovery under Arkansas law. As will be noted, this was not be the only problem with the administration of the Lindsey Cross Estate.

Before proceeding with a determination of the state's liability, the Claims Commission felt it necessary to give its take on the nature of segregation, Arkansas style.

The state in its composite wisdom has seen fit to create schools for both races and for both sexes commonly referred as Industrial Schools, where youths may be sent for correctional training. It is the custom to place negro supervisors over the negro children under the supposition that members of that race would be best to cope with the problem and give to their wards the best training available in order to prepare the inmates for worthy citizenship.

Notwithstanding the fact that black adolescent males had received almost no training at all, much less "the best training available," the irony of these proceedings is that Lester Gaines, the person who was actually accused of wrongdoing, was probably not within four hundred miles of Arkansas at the time of the commission's hearings. The Claims Commission was obviously unwilling to consider that a "proximate cause" of the fire also lay with the executive and legislative branches of state government because of their collective failure (despite being put on notice) to seek and appropriate funds to maintain a building that was known to be a firetrap. The commission acknowledged that "some evidence, partly hearsay, has been adduced concerning possible trouble with the wiring in the building, and there was other evidence that the building was old." But having named the elephant in the room, the commission said it was of no importance.

> Many [state] buildings housing school children much older than
> the building in question are being safely used every day, because the
> immediate dangers evident in them are sought out and corrected,
> or closely watched. If those in immediate charge of the respondent
> school had used the building to its best advantage, and had taken the
> necessary precautions in case of fire, no doubt all the inmates of the
> building would have been able to make their escape.

The assumptions that undergird the logic of the commission at this remove are hard to fathom. As stated earlier, the governor himself had admitted that the Wrightsville institution was "perhaps the worst" of the "firetraps" operated by the state. As noted, Lester Gaines had appeared before the Legislative Council and told them of the dilapidated condition of the dormitory that within a year was in flames, and it had done nothing. Given, as also previously noted, that the fire by all accounts appeared to have begun in the front of the building, the commission's conclusion that had "the necessary precautions" been taken all would have escaped, appears to be nothing less than a guess, and not particularly an educated one at that.

It was apparently much safer to blame "L.R. Gaines and his assistants for ignor[ing] their duty to their wards and lock[ing] up some

69 boys in one building without any way to escape, or without anyone nearby to watch over the safety of the boys." In fact, the governor himself had authorized or had been aware that the boys were locked in at night.

The commission also wrote that in addition, "The direct and proximate cause of the deaths of the boys was the failure to keep inside said dormitory buckets, water, or fire extinguishers . . . failure to conduct fire drills to be executed in the event of fire." Again, given that the fire appeared to have come from the ceiling, fire extinguishers and buckets of water and a fire drill would not have been of much use in combating a fire that had been building in an unobserved location.

To understand the impact of the proceedings on the Lindsey Cross Estate, one had to follow the path of the proceedings involved in the Estate of Willie Piggee. The commission awarded a total of $6,100 for this claim, granting the administrator for the Piggee family the sum of $2,500.00 "to compensate for the mental anguish, pain and suffering of the Decedent." Additionally, the commission awarded various amounts to individual Piggee family members "for the loss of companionship."

The applicable facts in the Piggee Estate also applied to the others. Thus, having established the liability of the state of Arkansas for the "wrongful death" of twenty-one boys, all that remained for the commission was to determine how much compensation to award the administrator on behalf of each estate and each lawful family member.

For the claim of W. J. Walker, as administrator of Lindsey Cross's estate, the Claims Commission awarded only a total of $3,400, which included damages for the following: (1) the sum of $2,500 "for the benefit of the decedent's estate to compensate for the mental anguish, pain, and suffering of the deceased; (2) the further sum of $600 for the use of Louvenia Lawrence, the mother, and the sum of $300 for the use of Charlie Cross, the father, to compensate them for their grief, loss of companionship and mental anguish because of the death of the decedent." The commission noted that "The Father, Charlie Cross, appears to have been away from his son most of the time for the past six years. Because of this fact, his award was materially less than the mother's."[22]

The only persons listed as heirs on the Claims Commission docket are Lindsey's mother and father, Luvenia (Long) Lawrence and Charlie Cross.[23] Even so, the failure to list Lindsey's two half-brothers and sister as heirs would not have prohibited them from receiving compensation for "loss of companionship" had either the administrator or their attorney brought this omission to the attention of the commission during the proceeding. For example, in deciding the claim of Rebecca Nelson, administrator of the Estate of Johnnie Tillison, who died in the NBIS fire, "the Commission finds that attorneys [Daggett and Daggett of Marianna] for claimant omitted the names of the sisters, the half sister, and half brothers from the complaint. The Commission will consider the complaint amended to include the names of the sisters, the half sister and the half brothers as Section 27–908 of the Statutes of Arkansas makes these children beneficiaries."[24]

Why no one called attention to the other family members of Lindsey Cross is inexplicable. Though who provided this information is not disclosed in the findings of the Claims Commission, the commission was at least aware that Charlie Cross was not present in the home "most of the time for the past six years." All anyone needed to do was to contact Ms. Long and ask her who her other children were and how they were related to Lindsey. In the other cases, the amounts awarded to siblings, including half siblings, were $300 each, not a substantial sum of money but a great deal to people as impoverished as Ms. Long and her children. Having three attorneys involved had cost her children $900 but that was only the beginning.

In his "Final report and Proposed Order of Distribution" filed on March 24, 1961, W. J. Walker, the administrator of the Estate of Lindsey Cross, swore before a notary on March 24, 1961, that "proper notice [to the distributees] has been given as required by law; that the names and addresses of Charlie Cross and Louvenia Cross [sic]" were those persons "entitled to distribution" of the Lindsey Cross estate; that Attorneys, Carl Langston and McMath, Leatherman and Woods, represented this estate and the heirs on contingent fee contracts of 40% of any amount recovered" and "that after the payment of attorneys' fees and costs, the Administrator proposes to pay $180 to Louvenia Cross and to pay the balance of said funds equally to Charlie Cross and Louvenia Cross."

The same day Probate Judge Guy Williams entered an Order of Final Distribution and signed the following order, finding "All distributes herein have waived notice of a hearing on said report; . . . The distribution proposed in the Administrator's report is in accordance with law; . . . *The attorneys' fee of 50%* are hereby allowed" (emphasis added).

Ms. Long would recall the day when a "tall white man" showed up at her door with a check for $1,000. "We didn't question it or know how to question it." When she took the check to be cashed at Square Deal Pawn Shop on Washington Avenue, Robert Itzkowitz asked her, "Is this all Faubus gave you for killing your son?" In fact, the governor had nothing to do with the amount of money any parent or relative received, but the point was well-taken.

Mistakes are common in legal pleadings; judges sometimes do not carefully read the orders they sign; however, the discrepancies in this proceeding went beyond clerical errors and showed the Arkansas legal profession in a bad light. Were the actions of the attorneys and judge involved in these proceedings carelessness, rank incompetence, or an indication of deliberate indifference and exploitation in a racist era? Whatever the answer, it is easy to understand the cynicism of the family of Lindsey Cross and the others who lost children in the fire.

Other questions remain. For a reason still unexplained, only twenty claims were filed. There is no claim listed for Joe Charles Crittenden of Blytheville, though he was one of the victims. His name appears on the list of the deceased boys made by the Arkansas State Police and is listed in the ledger of the Haven of Rest Cemetery, where the remains of fourteen of the boys were interred. The attorneys for the twenty claimants were all white law firms. Why no black attorneys represented the black claimants is still a puzzle.[25]

Ms. Long eventually bought a lot from Itzkowitz and began to build a house for her children. The wife of the white family for whom she was working as a maid in North Little Rock prevailed upon her husband, John Marshall, to help her. He, she recalls, "dug the foundation" for her, but "I dug the gas and the water lines myself and I sealed the walls up with pasteboard. I then took what was left of the money and finished the roof with tarpaper."[26] As adults, her sons Frank and Greg teased her that "it rained more inside the house than it did outside" because when the wind blew, water drained off nearby trees into the house. But at least someone had helped her dig the foundation.

CHAPTER NINE

Grand Jury

It is the courage to seek the truth and to speak it that can save us from the narcotic of self-deception. . . . It is a paradox of our time that those with power are too comfortable to notice the pain of those who suffer, and those who suffer have no power. To break out of this trap requires, as Elie Wiesel has put it, the courage to speak truth to power.

—**Daniel Goleman**, *Vital Lies, Simple Truth: The Psychology of Self-Deception*

It was not until the winter of 1960 that Frank Holt, the prosecuting attorney of Pulaski County, got around to investigating the Wrightsville fire. It was no surprise that he turned the matter of the fire over to the Pulaski County Grand Jury rather than make the decision himself whether to charge anyone.[1]

From a strictly legal standpoint, his choice was entirely appropriate. The Public Institutions Committee of the Pulaski County Grand Jury, which was assigned the investigation, had statutory authority to inquire into "conditions and management of public prisons within the respective counties." The notion that the racial composition of a grand jury must reflect the community and not simply the white power structure was a hard lesson to learn in Arkansas, whether it was in the Delta or the center of the state. Whether it was challenged during the litigation following the Elaine Race Massacres of 1919 or in 1968 following the race riot in Little Rock, the outcome would always be the same: the grand jury could not withstand scrutiny because of its composition.[2] As it would turn out, however, no one would question its makeup in 1960.

Once they got started, though, the members of the grand jury were doggedly thorough in investigating the fire. However, some of their conclusions would be questionable. Grand jury foreman R. C. Davis informed the press that the jurors would summon individuals "from the list of witnesses on the state police report of the fire which Governor Faubus handed to Prosecutor J. Frank Holt several months ago." The Pulaski County Grand Jury would end up calling thirty-two witnesses, including board members, employees, and fire inspectors, and it had available all the reports and investigations by the State Police and the board. Since grand jury proceedings are secret, and any leaks were apparently minor, only a few facts and rumors emerged. On January 21, 1960, the grand jury questioned Mary Gaines and six other witnesses. Five days later it called seven witnesses. For Fire Marshal W. C. Struebing, it was his second appearance. An *Arkansas Gazette* article on February 4 stated, "It was rumored that one of the witnesses the Jury is trying to call Tuesday is L.R. Gaines . . . [who] is reportedly in ill health living temporarily in Chicago."

The Public Institutions Committee visited Wrightsville on February 16, 1960, and claimed in its final report "that the school, under the direction of Superintendent Hemphill, is in a markedly sounder condition than it was before the tragic fire a year ago." Whether accurate or not, this opinion had nothing to do with the alleged guilt or innocence of Superintendent Gaines.

In submitting its final report on March 4, 1960, to Circuit Judge William Kirby, the Pulaski County Grand Jury noted that "the major and most time-consuming subject considered . . . was the tragic fire." "The new sleeping quarters for the boys," the report said, "is a very attractive but functional building that is fireproof. . . . Mr. Hemphill is enthusiastic about the school and his opportunity there. He is overflowing with ideas for improvement for the boys, including education, recreation and religious training." One familiar with the institution might have recalled, however, similar enthusiasm when Lester Gaines became superintendent in 1953.

As for the responsibility for the fire, the grand jury wrote,

The blame can be placed on lots of shoulders for the tragedy: the
Board of Directors to a certain extent, who might have pointed out
through newspaper and other publicity the extreme hazard and plight
of the school; the Superintendent and his staff, who perhaps continued
to do the best they could in a resigned fashion when they had nothing
to do with; the State Administration, one right after another through
the past years, who allowed the conditions to remain so disreputable;
the General Assembly of the State of Arkansas, who should have been
so ashamed of conditions that they would have previously allowed
sufficient money to have these conditions corrected; and finally on the
people of Arkansas, who did nothing about it.

The report was signed by three of the four men who served on
the Public Institutions Committee of the grand jury. Heading the
blue-ribbon list of names was banker B. Finley Vinson, who the
previous year had been part of the coalition to re-open the Little
Rock schools. In 1960 the business community still had no taste for
the kind of publicity that had occurred in 1957 and afterwards. The
Central High School Crisis and its aftermath had been every central Arkansas businessman's nightmare. Since 1957 industries had
avoided locating in Little Rock, and the business community had
taken note.

In 1993 Vinson sat down with historian John Kirk for an interview about the civil rights era and acknowledged that in his role
as chairman of the Little Rock Housing Authority he had worked
to keep the city segregated. "We built everything on it—we never
thought of building anything on this basis except segregation. That
was all over the country not just here . . . the city in all its actions
followed the people. The people were segregated. That's the way it
was."[3] True enough, the "people" were segregated, but the people
who made the decisions were white. In 1961 it would be the white
business community that took the lead in beginning negotiations

with a coalition of black activists who demanded an end to segregation in downtown Little Rock.[4] Tokenism would soon become the order of the day. A bit defensively, Vinson recalled that later he "put the first black on a bank board in Arkansas . . . and had the first black bank officer" in the state.[5]

Since the grand jury proceedings were secret, the reasons for its failure to indict a single person can only be a matter of speculation. Despite all the evidence against former superintendent Gaines, there were very practical reasons for an all-white grand jury not to hold him criminally responsible. Even a half-way competent attorney would have had a field day cross-examining state employees. The accounts of the trial would have made their way to the national media via wire services, once again shaming the state. After all, as mentioned, Gaines had appeared before the appropriate legislative committee and had laid out the problems with the dormitory. His lawyer could have claimed with justification that Wrightsville was so understaffed that it was impossible to prevent the fire from taking lives, assuming it started in the wiring as it most likely had. Not only did Gaines not have the resources to deal with a fire once it got started at Wrightsville, as mentioned, the governor himself had either ordered the boys to be locked in at night or had approved it, a situation that did not exist at the white boys school in Pine Bluff, where they had two house parents on duty all the time.

Though Orval Faubus had made no secret of his desire that Lester Gaines be criminally indicted, the governor and the legislature were fortunate that the grand jury chose not to be specific about their own failures to provide adequate funding to Wrightsville. The governor's immediate response to the grand jury's report was that he would need to take some time to review it before commenting. In fact, it appears that he reserved his public comments for his two self-published books, *Down from the Hills I* and *II*.

In the *Arkansas Gazette*, an editorial captioned "Arkansas's Lesson in Wrightsville Fire" claimed the lesson to be learned was to discover if "there are other Arkansas institutions vulnerable to similar horror today? . . . We must believe that Governor Faubus . . . has called in, or will soon call in responsible officials for an accounting of conditions in all institutions where human life is in the charge of the state." The *Gazette* seems to have forgotten that it had run a story the day after the fire in which the state hospital administration had warned of the disaster that would occur if a fire broke out. In summary, the *Gazette* seemed to be satisfied that no specific individual had been indicted and publicly thanked by name the members of the Public Institutions Committee for their work: "The forcefulness of their language should impress all of us with our responsibilities in these institutions and the people in them."[6]

By May 22, 1960, the date of the dedication of the new dormitory and other improvements at the Negro Boys Industrial School at a total cost of $150,000, a new civil rights era had dawned in central Arkansas. In March, students from Philander Smith College protesting segregation in Little Rock had staged two sit-ins in downtown Little Rock. Five had gotten arrested for their trouble but were bailed out of jail by the NAACP.[7] Elsewhere in the South, a new group called the Student Nonviolent Coordinating Committee had formed in Nashville, Tennessee, and on March 9, member James Lawson, a fervent apostle of nonviolence, spoke at the Dunbar Community Center in Little Rock. On April 15, Daisy Bates picketed along with students to protest segregation at three downtown eating places, most notably Woolworth's. Though the civil rights movement had started much earlier, the Student Nonviolent Coordinating Committee (SNCC) would provide much of the energy in Arkansas between 1960 and 1966.

The looming threat of more civil rights activity may well have prompted the governor's choice of words at the dedication site. Uncharacteristically emotional, Orval Faubus called for cooperation, citing the undeniable financial gains blacks had made during his tenure in office as a result of his ability to get through the legislature, as previously mentioned, increased welfare payments for the indigent elderly, raises for teachers, better highways, and the

University of Arkansas for Medical Sciences, which "serves all people alike."

"These things we did by working together," the governor said to a mostly black crowd estimated to be between three and four hundred people, "not by fighting, not by yielding to the agitators of whatever race or creed." Calling on the audience for continued support, he spoke of unity. The governor urged, "Let's continue to do the best job possible with these boys here" as if Wrightsville had been a first-rate institution during its entire existence and he had been responsible. "'So long as I am the governor of Arkansas . . . I will continue to do good for all people, no matter what the controversies that are started, no matter how they swirl around my head,' Mr. Faubus pledged emotionally."[8]

To be sure, "controversies" had taken a toll. In the 364 days since the fire, Orval Faubus hadn't always been able to disappear suddenly into one of his "holes" and emerge unscathed. As has been told many times, the plan to pack the Little Rock school board with his supporters had badly misfired. A coalition of his enemies led by the Women's Emergency Committee and joined by black voters had narrowly won a recall election and now controlled the Little Rock school board. The federal courts had ruled against him on the private school issue, and out of money, Raney High School had abruptly closed.

Central High School and the other high schools in Little Rock were open again after being shuttered all year. Today, the conventional narrative in Little Rock is that the forces of moderation had prevailed and the public school system had been saved. In 2016 one might challenge that view and argue that it was just beginning a protracted death.

In fact, in some telling ways, Wrightsville continued to be operated under a new superintendent as it had in the past. On March 25, 1961, the *Arkansas Gazette* reported that "an audit of the school showed that boys in custody there were working on a farm owned by Dr. T. J. Raney of Little Rock. There was no report on the earnings of inmates. When contacted about the matter, Raney said, "He didn't employ any of the boys directly." Rather, "his farm manager hired them under an agreement with the school" and the School's board had approved this arrangement." Raney professed not to know "what the boys were paid," saying "he paid the wages to the school."

As noted previously, renting the boys out as farm labor was not new. The boys had been employed by Raney and others before. A legislative audit on April 22, 1959, revealed that Raney was not the only employer, but the others were not listed. The boys picked and chopped cotton for Dr. Raney. According to the *Gazette*, "The School received half of the inmates' earnings in the form of feed and grain. The remainder was paid in cash which was credited to the boys. The audit showed the boys received $2 a day chopping cotton, from $1.70 to $2.50 for picking cotton and 80 cents each for baling hay."[9]

Since this practice was similar to peonage or debt slavery, it clearly made the Legislative Joint Auditing Committee nervous. During the Great Depression, *Time* magazine had run an article titled "Slavery in Arkansas." This had to do with "the practice of Delta planters taking convicted prisoners and working them on their plantations until their fines were paid off."[10] The practice was a bit different at Wrightsville, but the resulting exploitation was the same. Children were involved, but agriculture required labor, and prison environments like Wrightsville had plenty of it. This was perhaps too close for comfort for the legislature because the governor's friend T. J. Raney was involved. The *Arkansas Gazette* explained, "There was some question raised about the judgment of the [black] Boys School Board in sanctioning the practice but the Committee decided finally this was not its business." The governor seemed uninterested in the problem. Though Orval Faubus received these reports from the legislature, "the result," said a legislator with experience, "is that these lay [on the governor's desk] where they become dormant."[11]

Almost fifty years later, Howard Lee Nash—who had been fifteen years old in 1959—recalled in a telephone interview his experiences both before and after the fire. Sent to Wrightsville in February 1959, he'd had no parental supervision. His father was in jail and his mother was living in New Jersey. Confined at the NBIS for "three to five" months for fighting at J. C. Cook High School in the nearby town of Wrightsville, Nash remembers loading hay and putting it in a barn for Dr. Raney. Tall for his age, he had been selected for this project with boys older than himself. Before this day was out, he fell out of a speeding truck and broke both legs. He was taken to Children's Hospital in Little Rock where he recuperated before being sent back to the institution to finish his sentence. Like the others, he had been able to escape during the fire by crawling out a window and claims to still bear a scar from that night. "We went out the window. . . . Wasn't nobody answering the door."

During his time at Wrightsville, Nash said he had gotten about "five or six whippings." He said boys were whipped "if you wet the bed, if you didn't pick enough cotton, if you got to fighting, if you tried to run off." He said he was held down by other inmates and hit with a "big, old strap" as wide as your hand . . . give you ten or fifteen licks . . . had boys hold you down if you wouldn't [stay down] . . . strap tore your butt up . . . didn't give you nothing for it . . . whipping would break the skin. Couldn't sit 'cause the skin was broke. Under-clothes would stick [to your skin]."

Nash said he had no contact with Lester Gaines but did recall Wilson Hall, saying he remembers Hall locking them in at night. Nash said he thought he and another employee rotated this duty.[12]

Nash's account of punishment was confirmed by Alvin Peters. He and a brother ran off to Chicago but were tracked down and brought back to experience "whipping night." During an emotional telephone interview, Peters acknowledged he had begun to cry and said it was the first time he had done so since the fire. He said the whippings were more brutal under Superintendent Hemphill.[13]

Most white Arkansans, including the governor, professed not to see that their treatment of African Americans as having anything to do with morality. "It is my opinion that the Negroes have not been especially discriminated against," Faubus wrote to a Wisconsin man on July 16, 1964, just days after President Lyndon Johnson had gone on national television and made race relations a moral issue in a way no southern politician had ever done. Upon signing the 1964 Civil Rights Act on July 2, Lyndon Johnson had said, "The reasons for racial discrimination . . . are deeply embedded in history, tradition, and the nature of man. . . . But it cannot continue. The Constitution, the principles of freedom and morality all forbid such unequal treatment." Yet in the president's view, the legacy of the past was more than "unequal treatment." Black poverty was caused by "the devastating heritage of long years of slavery and a century of oppression, hatred, and injustice." Their poverty could only remind blacks "of their oppression. For the white they are a constant reminder of guilt."[14]

The governor would have none of it. In the letter to the Wisconsin correspondent, he probably spoke for the average white Arkansan when he wrote, "Usually people get in this world about what they have earned and what they deserve. Whenever the Negro improves his life *morally*, and especially in the *moral* field does he need improvement, educationally, physically, and otherwise, then much of the so-called prejudice will fade away and disappear"[15] (emphases added).

Though Faubus himself often cheated and lied to gain political advantage, perhaps since he considered politics a "grand game" where success went to the most cunning and "slick," morality did not factor into it. As the legal pressure increased on the state dramatically to desegregate its facilities during his next three terms in office, Faubus concentrated on trying to improve institutions like the Negro Boys Industrial School as if it were still possible to forestall integration. Now, during his fifth term, the state of Arkansas was finally spending the money to install a water main at the school, although not in time to prevent the destruction of the boys' infirmary by fire after 1959. According to Superintendent Hemphill, the fire had started in the attic of the infirmary, and it had burned before the Little Rock fire department could save it. Had the water main "been completed, it might have been possible to save the building, the superintendent said. Governor Faubus this week took $50,000 out of his emergency fund to be spent on housing at the facility."[16]

As was becoming increasingly obvious after the passage of the Civil Rights Act of 1964, it would be only a matter of time before litigation or its threat would be enough to desegregate all state institutions, but white Arkansas under Orval Faubus continued to resist the inevitable. In 1965 Faubus tried to make the state capitol cafeteria a private club. This degrading effort resulted in SNCC workers being clubbed and gassed during a peaceful demonstration. The governor justified his decision by saying, "If you give in to them on this, there will be something else."[17]

A 1964 African American graduate of Yale Law School, native Arkansan John W. Walker, among other litigants, began filing civil rights lawsuits in federal court in Arkansas soon after he was admitted to the bar. With the assistance of the NAACP Legal Defense Fund, he would become the premier civil rights attorney in the state. A 1966 class action suit Walker filed on behalf of Lincoln County residents Nona Mae George and her minor son, Roy Lee Lewis, straightforwardly alleged that assigning or sentencing "Negro" juveniles to Wrightsville on the basis of race or color pursuant to Arkansas statutes violated their constitutional rights to equal protection and due process. It was a case in which the law was so clear that upon appeal by the state to the US Court of Appeals for the Eighth Circuit, the court summarily cut through the procedural issues raised by the state and ruled that the Arkansas statutes requiring segregation of juveniles "are clearly unconstitutional" and "under no circumstance should race become a determinative factor in assignment." The state would continue to attempt to delay integration at Wrightsville, and it was not until 1968 that a final order was implemented.[18]

CHAPTER TEN

Lessons Learned and Not Learned

Orval Faubus appears to have been telling the truth when he informed the press that Superintendent Gaines had gotten Wilson Hall and Lee Austin to fabricate a story about their duties and whereabouts on the night of the fire. As mentioned, a close reading of newspaper accounts shows that Lester Gaines revealed on the morning of the fire that he had inexplicably assigned no employee to spend the night at the older boys' dormitory, a statement he never satisfactorily explained. Though clearly exhausted and drained by the events and his responsibilities, each succeeding explanation he gave was a contradiction of the last one.

Furthermore, in a taped interview with Frank Lawrence almost fifty years later, the surviving members of the Wilson Hall family were adamant that their father did not leave the house the night of the fire. While Frank Lawrence had not made the Hall offspring aware that in answer to a question at the hearing over the weekend of March 7–8, their mother had told the board members that her husband *had* left the house that night around 3 a.m., Mrs. Hall's next response to the board substantially invalidated her prior answer to the board. Having just answered that she knew her husband did leave the house around three, Mrs. Hall's claim that she did not know that her husband had been assigned to check on Austin during this period would not have been credible. Had her husband, Wilson Hall, actually been assigned to go each night at 9 p.m. and 3 a.m. to check to make sure Lee Austin was at the boys' dormitory for the duration of P. R. Banks's hospitalization, she would, of course, have known. It appears she was covering for her husband in her first answer and trying not to implicate herself in her second. Little Rock attorney Annette Hall remembers her mother saying to her father, "Wilson, why are you doing that [telling this story]?"[1] Additionally, in an e-mail about Wilson Hall's behavior the night of the fire, Frank Lawrence acknowledged that one of the Hall offspring told him that their father had met with Faubus.[2]

Though most of the employees who resided on the grounds of the institution gave statements to the board supporting Lester Gaines's version of events, they appear to have been reporting what they knew. In fact, none of them would have necessarily been aware if Gaines, as time wore on and Banks remained ill, had told Hall and Austin to alternate putting the boys to bed. As mentioned, what is not certain is how much difference it would have made, since the fire marshal's report was never released or found. Thus there is no conclusive evidence of how the fire started, or where it had begun, and how controllable it would have been once it had been detected. Most of the bodies were found at the back of the dormitory, suggesting that the fire had begun near the front door.

It is unclear whether Lester Gaines tried to intimidate any other employees. Based on their statements at the hearing and the letter they signed in support of him, most employees appear to have been quite loyal to him, even, as mentioned, going so far as to resign when he was fired. It seems plausible that Gaines would draw up a work schedule each week, but since it has never been found, it cannot be said with certainty what the duties of Austin and Hall were while Banks was in the hospital.

Employee Dorothy Mattison has no personal recollection of signing the document supporting Gaines that appeared in the press and only vague memories of the aftermath of the fire. On the other hand, she had no negative memories of Lester Gaines, nor did she remember that he tried to intimidate or influence her or her husband.[3] Nor is it beyond doubt that Lester Gaines was actually on the campus the night of the fire. At the same time, it is not certain that he was even required to be.

Though his decision not to require an employee to be present at night at the dormitory is inexplicable, Lester Gaines had the responsibility for running a badly understaffed firetrap of an institution that had been virtually ignored by individuals and institutions with the power to make a difference. He had called the legislature's attention to the condition of the dormitory, and no one had listened. Yet no matter how many reasons he might have offered, one wonders how he could ever forget his first inspection visit to the Wrightsville institution, where he and others heard the then superintendent describe a fire in the "little boys" dormitory, which also was locked from the outside.

Did Orval Faubus have any culpability for the deaths of the boys? During his more than two terms in office before the fire, the governor had done very little for the institution. As one of the out-of-state letters suggested, had he spent the time and energy trying to get an appropriation for repairs at Wrightsville that he spent confounding his political enemies and trying to keep the Little Rock schools segregated, perhaps there would have been no fire. As mentioned, he was aware the boys were locked in at night and knew the security arrangements at the older boys' dormitory.

In *Ruled by Race* (2009), I argued that "nothing illustrated Orval Faubus's cynical use of race than his behavior during the aftermath of the ... fire."[4] Before and after the fire, the governor used the issue of race to bedevil his political enemies. With his history of lying and telling half-truths to justify his actions, Faubus was often successful in deflecting criticism, thus escaping blame and responsibility for much of his six terms in office. By becoming personally involved in the "investigation," the governor was following a pattern of behavior that had served him well politically.

However, in retrospect, without more evidence, it is impossible to know to any reasonable degree of certainty the governor's motives for behaving as he did vis-à-vis the fire. I believe that a reassessment of the governor's actions regarding the fire is in order.

While it still appears that for political reasons Faubus intended to deflect attention from his failure to address the needs of the

Wrightsville institution, arguably, his behavior during the immediate aftermath of the fire was, on its face, appropriate. He took immediate responsibility for getting to the bottom of the controversy about whether or not the actions of employees caused the deaths of the boys. Had he ignored the role of his superintendent, certainly he would have come in for legitimate criticism. Though in the category of "closing the barn door after the animals had run off," by announcing his intention to sell excess farm land to the highest bidder, he made sure that legislative action would be taken as promptly as possible to rebuild and fireproof the dormitory. As the chief executive who appointed the board to question employees about the fire, he was understandably unhappy by the failure of his chairman, Alfred Smith, to ask more probing questions and the board's recommendation that there be no consequences except a scolding of one employee. In light of Smith's incomplete questioning and the board's recommendations of nothing more than a slap on the wrist, any governor would have been justified in rejecting its conclusions and recommendations. To be sure, the manner in which Faubus did so raises questions about the procedure and secrecy of his investigation. His statement about an unnamed "colored friend" escorting two black employees to the governor's mansion to be interrogated by him leaves one wondering if the employees felt they were being coerced by the governor. Yet Faubus could claim, as mentioned, that since his suspicions had been aroused, he had gone further and expanded his investigation that led to the revelation of other wrongdoing on the part of his superintendent and wife. In light of this information, his recommendation to his board that Lester and Mary Gaines and her brother be terminated seems more like an appropriate response than a deliberate ploy to blame others. Years later, in his two books defending his tenure in office, Faubus would again contend that "someone" should have been criminally prosecuted.[5] His conclusions seem defensible even if one ignores how little he had done in the years before the fire and how much corruption he overlooked by his white cronies during his six terms as governor. Whether Lester Gaines and others should have been convicted is a question that has no easy answer.

Though it goes against the settled opinions of those southerners and northerners, white and black, who point fingers at Orval Faubus for the travesty at Central High School and its aftermath, he will always remain an enigma. In his highly praised biography of Orval Faubus, Roy Reed writes that after six years of work on the book and "hundreds of hours listening to his subject and looking him in the eye," he

> is forced to admit that Orval Eugene Faubus is more mysterious now than when the process began.... He appears still in my mind, even after his death, as an insoluble mixture of cynicism and compassion, of guile and grace, of wickedness and goodness. I have observed his life off and on for forty years, and I don't know whether he was good or evil, or even whether those are the choices. There was a time when I knew. But that was long ago and I was young.[6]

This judgment of Faubus by Reed, a dyed-in-the-wool Arkansan whose reputation as a highly experienced and sophisticated political observer not only of the South, but also the world scene as a national and foreign correspondent for the *New York Times*,[7] has disappointed those who expected Reed to add his imprimatur to the governor's demonization, which began with his decision to prevent the Little Rock Nine from entering Central High School. Yet Reed's candid admission of his inability to categorize Faubus as either good or evil or a mixture of both or neither comports with the since-the-world-began difficulty of unraveling human motivation.

As long as he remained governor, Orval Faubus would be haunted by the fire. On April 7, 1966, he wrote Superintendent Hemphill, whom he had appointed seven years earlier, the following: "I know we have put up a lot of new buildings at the Negro Boys' School, and some of the dormitories are fireproof. With all the new buildings we have constructed there, do we still have some boys who are housed in wooden barracks? If so, please give me a letter of explanation? [sic]"

Hemphill replied, "We do not have any wooden barracks on the premises. Some of the younger students are housed in a one-story brick veneer which was constructed in 1930."[8]

As mentioned, listed last by the Pulaski County Grand Jury of those responsible for the condition of the institution at Wrightsville "are the people of Arkansas who did nothing about it." Though intended by the authors as a moral indictment for the neglect of a single, specific institution, this unvarnished pronouncement of blame presented white Arkansans, had they wished, the opportunity to explore the depth of their responsibility for their implementation of a system of white supremacy that was pervasive throughout the state. Specifically, were the deaths of the twenty-one boys at the Negro Boys Industrial School merely an isolated, though deeply regrettable, case of long-term negligence? Or was it one of the most horrific examples of the consequences of the implementation of a culture and political system whose operating principles, formally and informally, were designed for the convenience, material, and emotional benefit of whites and the subjugation of blacks?

While the lack of available evidence prohibits a decisive determination of facts about the motivation of those individually responsible for the operation and management of the Negro Boys Industrial School from Orval Faubus on down, the implementation of the broader aspects of white supremacy, particularly in the funding and management of separate institutions for blacks and whites, is relevant here. The woeful history of the Negro Boys Industrial School and also the astonishing disparities between white and black institutions during the era of Jim Crow were a consequence of the commitment of whites to maintain and implement white supremacy for as long as politically possible. In other words, the conditions at Wrightsville and other black institutions and the attitudes of the white power structure toward them were a product of "structural racism," which scholars Keith Lawrence and Terry Keleher have defined as the normalization and legitimization of an array of dynamics, historical, cultural, institutional, and interpersonal that routinely advantages whites while producing cumulative and adverse chronic outcomes for people of color. Structural racism encompasses the entire system of white supremacy, diffused and infused in all aspects of society including our history, culture, politics and economics.

The history of the Negro Boys Industrial School in most of its aspects serves as a template for structural racism regarding other black institutions in Arkansas during this era of white supremacy. "Key indicators are inequalities in power, access, opportunities, and policy impacts . . . it is a system of hierarchy and inequity, primarily characterized by white supremacy—the preferential treatment, privileges and power for white people at the expense of black, latino, pacific islander, native American and other racially oppressed people."[9]

Though by 1959 some Americans of African descent in Arkansas were in "charge" of black institutions and exercised real authority over education in certain areas, they operated in a world sharply constrained by the politics of white supremacy, which dictated "inequalities in power, access, opportunities, and policy impacts" mentioned in the above definition. Thus, the conditions at Wrightsville were not the result of "mere" negligence over a long period of time but are more accurately characterized by systematic inequality, and in the case of the older boys at the Negro Boys Industrial School, there was a consistent intention to limit their opportunities to farm labor.

As mentioned, John Gould Fletcher had spoken for most whites when he forthrightly acknowledged that white southerners meant to dominate and control "their" black populations. As time went on, and the spotlight of history fell again more heavily upon the South, some white southerners began to be shamed, a consequence that ethics philosopher Kwame Anthony Appiah contends has been effective in banishing some behavior found reprehensible by the world at large, including foot binding in China and the slave trade in England. In his book *The Honor Code: How Moral Revolutions Happen* (2010), he suggests that "the heart of the psychology of honor—the giving and receiving of respect—is ... in every normal human being, however [the degree to which they are] enlightened and advanced."[10]

Throughout much of their history beginning in the twentieth century and coming forward into the twenty-first, many white Arkansans have been embarrassed and defensive about the state's image as a backward and racist culture. However white supremacy was defended, its most visible historical manifestations—lynching, the images of violence, and the expressions of hatred at Central High School—were cause for shame and finger-pointing. Many white Arkansans wanted the respect of others outside the South, and the deaths of the twenty-one boys coming after the Little Rock High crisis of 1957 once again had a shaming effect, or in the words of the grand jury report, should have made the legislature "ashamed." But in this era, even the most concerned white Arkansans would make only cosmetic changes to the established order. Rather than confront their long and often brutal history of white supremacy and acknowledge the truth of President Lyndon Johnson's words in 1964, it fell to a white Methodist minister to articulate in a never-published memoir of this period the static views of this era. As the longest-serving director of the Arkansas Council on Human Relations, a nonprofit organization formed in 1954 out of the Southern Regional Council, which sought to facilitate the transition to a desegregated society, Nat Griswold had a unique understanding of his fellow Arkansans in this period. While "the Arkansas Council on Human Relations has been credited with being an organization that was instrumental in desegregating schools and businesses,"[11] Griswold saw little change in the fundamental attitudes of his white members that at one time numbered about a thousand individuals. Calling his unpublished memoir of this period "The Second Reconstruction," he wrote,

The Arkansas Council on Human Relations, a membership group during the fearful "silent years" [1957 and afterwards] associated together just over two hundred in the state. When tokenism in desegregation became preferable to possible violence, this group came to be more respected and had as many as one thousand members in 1965. But as a political force their number never challenged seriously officials or politicians.

Therefore, an observer might honestly conclude that the activities of these dissenters to the standing order primarily was a therapy to the individuals. It enabled them to live with themselves. Such an appraiser might point out that most of them never visualized serious changes in the existing order of segregated institutions, never clearly broke with that order. They only sought to soften its glaring cruelties. It can be documented that some supporters of reform organizations were at the same time primary props to the old.[12]

The many Arkansans who had blamed Orval Faubus for the way he handled the school desegregation crisis in Little Rock and the negative publicity resulting from it rarely questioned the consequences of their own complicity and roles in the maintenance of white supremacy. In constructing a narrative of the past, it has been much easier for white southerners to scapegoat specific individuals than to accept individual and collective responsibility for the creation and perpetuation of a society so relentlessly hostile and destructive of their common humanity and values.

On March 5, 2011, the governor of Arkansas signed an official proclamation declaring "Arkansas Negro Boys Industrial School Fire Remembrance Day." At the request of African American state senator Joyce Elliot, the proclamation signed by Governor Mike Beebe noted that the Wrightsville institution was established "in 1923 during the infamous era of racial segregation of public schools, public places, and public transportation, restrooms, restaurants, and drinking fountains; as well as the United States Military."[13]

Though this gesture was appreciated, family members and their supporters have wanted much more than a proclamation and a photo op with the governor. On March 5, 2009, the fiftieth anniversary of the fire, thirty or so family members and supporters had gathered at Haven of Rest Cemetery to remember their loved ones but also in the hope that the state of Arkansas would assist them in several matters related to the deaths of the boys, including finally identifying their remains. To this end, the group filed incorporation papers with the secretary of state's office as the ASH Foundation, ASH being an acronym for Arkansas's Secret Holocaust, according to Frank Lawrence. A brief memorial service was followed by a press conference on the steps of the state capitol. Frank Lawrence told the media, "Nothing has been done in order to get closure for these families. We are asking the United States Department of Justice to open the first cold case of its kind in the state of Arkansas." He was appealing for action under the 2007 federal legislation known as the Emmett Till Unsolved Civil Rights Crime Act.[14]

Peggy Duncan, a white woman then a resident of North Little Rock, is listed as "Chief Financial Officer" of ASH. She explained her involvement with the group in an interview three years later: "I'm ashamed of what happened. I was raised by a very dear, dear black woman. I think Johnnie would turn over in her grave if she knew I didn't do anything. . . . My mother was not well, and [she] worked for my family—spanked my butt when it needed to be spanked and patted me on the head when I needed to be patted on the head." Duncan had joined ASH after reading a cover story about the fire in the "Arkansas Times."[15] She was incensed that nothing had been done for the families of the boys. Central High had been given its rightful place in history. But no student died at Central. Why not deal with Wrightsville? Family members wanted authorities to pay to exhume the remains of the twenty-one children so they could be properly identified. They wanted a monument to acknowledge what had been done to their boys. Instead, the fire had been ignored for fifty years. Thus far, beyond a spate of publicity and the proclamation, nothing has been accomplished.

Ardecy and Archie Gyce, who lost their brother Amos in the fire, typify family members who have question after question about the fire and its consequences. The unidentifiable remains of an individual that their mother, now deceased, chose that horrible morning to say was her son and their brother, are buried at the family plot in Woodson, a town near Wrightsville. The odds are, of course, high that what is in the coffin are not the remains of their treasured older brother Amos, who once cut off Ardecy's hair when she was five so he and his brothers wouldn't be seen playing with a girl. Was Amos guilty of anything that should have landed him in the Negro Boys Industrial School? Even today his brother and sister believe he would have been exonerated by his best friend, who could have explained that Amos had permission to remove a sum of money from his father's safe. What did Amos do to deserve the whippings and being sent to bed hungry in those few months he was at Wrightsville? Why did the family only receive a thousand dollars for his death? Where was Lester Gaines when the fire started? According to Archie Gyce, there were stories that he was as far away as St. Louis. Did Lester Gaines get to receive his pension as a state employee, as Ms. Gyce contends?

In one way, however, Ardecy Gyce is not typical of other family members. In the military for twenty years, she says she has spent around $2,000 on the efforts to get ASH up and running as an organization, and now nothing was happening. Both Ardecy and Archie Gyce, believe, as many do, that the actual story of the fire is still hidden.[16]

◆ ◆ ◆

In the age of the Internet, conspiracy theories abound on every controversial subject, and Frank Lawrence has a number of his own about the fire. In 2008 he shared them in an interview. As suggested in the first chapter and restated here, the belief that the state of

Arkansas "swept the fire under the rug" is shared by a number of people, particularly Arkansans of African descent. Lawrence suggested
that the fire may have been tied to the Little Rock desegregation crisis and that the Ku Klux Klan might have been responsible for the
fire. He argued the media may have been tipped off in advance that
the dormitory was going to be burned; alternatively, he stated that
the fire might have been set deliberately so that the school's acreage
could be sold cheaply to Orval Faubus's wealthy friend and personal
physician, Dr. T. J. Raney. He also claimed that Orval Faubus, Alfred
Smith, and Lester Gaines may have received payment for the work
done by the boys on the acreage that was being rented to Raney.
He suggested that survivor Roy Davis was transferred to Cummins
prison from Wrightsville because he refused to answer questions
about the fire and be intimidated by board chairman Alfred Smith.
He stated that the coffins at Haven of Rest are empty.[17]

Though I have found no evidence that confirms these theories,
I give credit to Lawrence for insisting that the deaths of the boys
receive the historical attention they deserve. Equally important is
the research he did, which I fully credit in the acknowledgments
section. In 2012 closure still eluded Frank Lawrence. Still insisting
that the remains of the fourteen boys, including his brother, were
never buried at Haven of Rest Cemetery, in 2012 he contacted the
Arkansas Archeological Survey to request that it use recent advances
in technology (radar) to determine the location of the remains. The
Haven of Rest Cemetery was then under receivership and managed
by the state of Arkansas. A large plaque at the location of the caskets
at one time said to be visible from the Twelfth Street border of the
gravesite has been stolen or removed.

The state Securities Office has jurisdiction under state law over
these matters and has detailed records and graphs documenting
the location within Haven of Rest of the fourteen caskets (Lot 99A
Carver Section, spaces 1–14). The remains of each boy is "identified" by name and number.[18] As mentioned, the difficulty, of course,

is that when the remains were first collected and taken to various burial facilities, they could not be identified, so any names purporting to be matched with remains have been assigned arbitrarily.

There is no substantial evidence that the fourteen coffins at Haven of Rest do not contain remains of children in the location identified by the Arkansas Securities Department. One may believe, of course, that state authorities and others colluded among themselves immediately after the fire to dispose of the remains, but no one has come forward with evidence to prove this is the case. None of the above lessens the pain of surviving family members who go to bed each night not even knowing where the boy that was taken from them is buried.

In my view, the entire history of the Negro Boys Industrial School was an example of the way white supremacy was implemented to meet the perceived needs of the dominant group. The "glaring cruelties" at Wrightsville were occasionally ameliorated by paternalism and acts of kindness by employees and others, beginning with the selection of Tandy Coggs as the superintendent. At its worst, its history ranged from negligence to "deliberate indifference" and possibly negligent homicide.

Finally, the sad story of the Arkansas Negro Boys Industrial School is a case study of the failure of Arkansans to come to terms with their historical commitment to white supremacy. As for the present era, anyone who regularly has kept up with the Arkansas juvenile justice system since the 1959 fire at Wrightsville cannot claim to be surprised by the reports of racial violence and intimidation that have been an ongoing feature of massive incarceration. In a judicial environment that has outlawed de jure segregation in public facilities, the "school-to-prison pipeline" for the poorest and least educated black Americans continues to run full throttle in Arkansas and throughout the nation and has had its own consequences for race relations.[19] Today in 2017, nine life-size statues of the nine students who desegregated Central High School grace the lawn at the state capitol. There are, of course, no statues of the boys who died in the fire. For the cynical, arguably, the statues of the Little Rock Nine are a cruel irony for those who are familiar today with the increasingly bitter and possibly futile struggle to maintain a credible, desegregated public school system in Arkansas.[20]

Notes

Introduction

Story L. Matkin-Rawn, "'We Fight for the Rights of Our Race': Black Arkansans in the Era of Jim Crow" (PhD diss., University of Wisconsin at Madison, 2009), 175. Scholars have documented that white southerners depended on northern philanthropic assistance from the Rosenwald and Slater Funds and others for much of black school construction.

1. *Arkansas State Press*, March 20, 1959. Unsigned editorials were written by L. C. Bates.

2. Grif Stockley, *Daisy Bates: Civil Rights Crusader from Arkansas* (Jackson: University Press of Mississippi, 2005).

3. While the concept of "race" has no scientific meaning or validity and thus is rightly dismissed by academics as an "artificial construct," the word's significance for past- and present-day relations between "blacks" and "whites" is indisputable. I state in *Ruled by Race: Black/White Relations in Arkansas from Slavery to the Present* (Fayetteville: University of Arkansas Press, 2008), 462n16, "I have chosen to characterize the events in this history as having a racial significance because that is how most Arkansans, white and black, have viewed 'race' relations and still, in fact, view them."

4. Grif Stockley, "The Twenty-One Deaths Caused by the 1959 Fire at the Negro Boys Industrial School: An Isolated Case of 'Neglect' or an Instance of Racial Violence?," in *Race and Ethnicity in Arkansas: New Perspectives*, ed. John A. Kirk, 74 (Fayetteville: University of Arkansas Press 2014). See also Stockley, *Ruled by Race*, Introduction, xv.

5. Carl H. Moneyhon, "David O. Dodd, the 'Boy Martyr of Arkansas': The Growth and Use of a Legend," *Arkansas Historical Quarterly* 74, no. 3 (Autumn 2015): 203–30.

Chapter One: The Charred Remains of Children

1. This heroic effort to alert the other boys, however brief, was not a self-serving account by these two survivors. When William Blanchard, age fifteen,

from Snow Lake in Desha County in the Arkansas Delta on the other side of the state, opened his eyes that morning, "It was hot [and] there was a lot of smoke," he said. He, too, saw "flames were dipping below the ceiling," adding that "two sergeants," Charles Meadows from El Dorado and Arthur Ray Poole, "were waking up the boys." *Arkansas Gazette*, March 6, 1959.

2. Ibid.

3. *Chicago Defender* (national edition), March 14, 1959.

4. *Arkansas Democrat*, March 6, 1959.

5. *Chicago Defender* (national edition), March 14, 1959.

6. *New York Times* (national edition), March 6, 1959.

7. Indeed, these statements, given in interviews by reporters the same morning, would, from a legal perspective, have satisfied the universal rules for trustworthiness in the American judicial system had it been necessary, for example, to introduce them into evidence as exceptions to the rule that prohibits hearsay testimony. They would have likely been admitted as "excited utterances," that is, spontaneous comments, made near or at the time of the event, and in some cases as admissions against their own interest.

8. *Arkansas Democrat*, March 5, 1959.

9. *Arkansas Times*, February 28, 2008.

10. James Watson, interview by Grif Stockley, September 14, 2011, Grif Stockley Papers (location to be determined).

11. Fire Station #13 Log, Frank Lawrence File, Grif Stockley Papers.

12. *Arkansas Democrat*, March 6, 1959.

13. However one interprets the term *cover-up*, in no way was the initial coverage of the fire minimized. A headline from the front page of the March 6, 1959, *Arkansas Gazette* reads, "Wrightsville Holocaust State's Worst." While the term *Holocaust*, of course, refers primarily to the murder of six millions Jews by the Nazis in World War II, it is a term that endures regarding the boys' deaths. As of 2012 on file at the Arkansas secretary of state's office, a listing of a nonprofit corporation in good standing is titled ASH Foundation, ASH being an acronym for Arkansas's Secret Holocaust, an organization founded by some of the family members of the deceased boys and their supporters.

14. "Confidential Investigation by Board," Orval E. Faubus Papers, box 302, folder 12, Special Collections, University of Arkansas Libraries, Fayetteville.

15. Mike Lindsey72@aol.com, e-mail message to Grif Stockley, January 14, 2008, quoting from transcript of interview with Ken McKee.

16. *Arkansas State Press*, March 20, 1959. Unsigned editorials were all written by L. C. Bates. Grif Stockley Papers. The names and hometowns of the fourteen boys whose ashes were placed in a common grave at the Haven of Rest Cemetery were Charles R. Thomas, Little Rock; Frank Barnes, Lake Village; Charles

White, Malvern; Johnny Tillison, LaGrange; Jessie Carpenter Jr., Fountain City [Hill?]; Joe Charles Crittenden, Blytheville; John Daniels, El Dorado; Carl E. Thornton, North Little Rock; Willie C. Horner, North Little Rock; Lindsey Cross, North Little Rock; R. D. Brown, Emerson; Edward Tolston, Wilmot; Cecil Preston, Blytheville; and Roy Chester Powell, Forrest City. Haven of Rest Ledger Sheet, Grif Stockley Papers. The names and hometowns of the seven other victims were Roy Hegwood, El Dorado; Amos Gyce, Woodson; John Alfred George, North Little Rock; O. F. Meadows, El Dorado; Willie Lee Williams, Helena; Willie Piggie, DeWitt; and Henry Daniel, Little Rock. The ages of the boys who died in the fire ranged from fifteen to eighteen, according to the *Arkansas Democrat*, March 5, 1959.

17. Arkansas Gazette, March 6, 1959.

18. Ibid.

19. Greg Lawrence, telephone interview by Grif Stockley, November 5, 11, 2009, Grif Stockley Papers. It was Greg Lawrence who remembered that the minister would come pick them up for church.

20. Cary Bradburn, *On the Opposite Shore: The Making of North Little Rock* (Marceline, MO: Walsworth Printing, 2004), 172.

21. The account of Lindsey's arrest and commitment to the NBIS derives from my interviews with Ms. Long. However, in a statement made for the documentary film her son Frank Lawrence was making, Ms. Long said that "my boy never did get no trial." In my view, the question of what happened to Lindsey Cross and the involvement of his mother after his arrest and before he was committed to the Negro Boys Industrial School is a matter of speculation and not capable of being definitively resolved at this remove in time. The North Little Rock Police Department does not maintain arrest records fifty years old. Not only are proceedings in Arkansas juvenile court closed, they were primarily administrative and not judicial in nature. In that era, juvenile proceedings all over the United States lacked the formal due process procedures of criminal cases. It would not be until 1967 in the case of *In Re Gault*, 387 U.S. 1 (1967) that the US Supreme Court would require that most due process procedures required in criminal courts be applied to juvenile proceedings. It so happens that the author brought the case in 1987 in which the Arkansas Supreme Court declared unconstitutional the juvenile system in operation at the time of the 1959 fire. *Walker v. Arkansas Dept. of Human Services*.

22. Howard Nash, telephone interview by Grif Stockley and Frank Lawrence. June 19, 2009, Grif Stockley Papers.

23. "Registration Record, Negro Boys Industrial School Wrightsville, Arkansas." The ledger begins in 1930 and was used until 1978, even after it was no longer a segregated facility. Grif Stockley Papers.

24. At times the mother of Lindsey Cross would give her last name as "Long" but also as "Lawrence," perhaps as a way of identifying with her son Frank Lawrence's project, which had it come to fruition, would have put her at the center of the controversy. Though in some instances her son sought to help direct her responses, it was clear she approved of his efforts to make a film about the fire.

25. "Frank Lawrence File," Grif Stockley Papers, "The century old Hubble Funeral Home . . ." The issue of whether the remains of Lindsey Cross were ultimately transferred to the casket for burial at Haven of Rest would become grounds for controversy almost fifty years later. Chapter Ten lists the contentions made by Frank Lawrence.

26. "Families of 21 who burned to death plead for investigation," http://pbcommercial.com/articles/2009/0306news2.txt.

27. Ms. Long, whose first name was sometimes spelled "Louvenia," was in her eighties when I interviewed her on two different occasions. One of these was a telephone interview. My other interview was at her home in North Little Rock. Her son Frank Lawrence was present for the latter interview. On both days, Ms. Long's memory was not the best. On occasion her son would try to help her remember events the day he was present. She had previously been interviewed by her son, who had begun to make a documentary about the fire. Another source of information about Ms. Long's past is Lawrence himself, whom I interviewed over two days at the Butler Center for Arkansas Studies in Little Rock as part of the digital AV/AR Ruled by Race Project. While an important source of information, Frank Lawrence's account of what he said about events in his mother's life differs in some details from what Ms. Long told me. For example, Frank Lawrence states in his interview that his mother had dropped out of school in the sixth grade. Ms. Long told me she left school in the ninth grade. Ms. Luvenia Long, telephone interview by Grif Stockley, October 19, 2009. Notes of this interview are part of the Grif Stockley Papers.

28. Josephine Strickland, telephone interview by Grif Stockley, November 10, 2009, Grif Stockley Papers.

29. Ibid., January 16, 2010.

30. Registry of NBIS, 57, Grif Stockley Papers. Lindsey's age was given in the NBIS registry as fourteen.

31. Paula J. Casey, "Arkansas Juvenile Courts: Do Lay Judges Satisfy Due Process in Delinquency Cases?," 6 UALR L. Review, 501, 503 (1983).

32. John Graves, *Town and Country: Race Relations in an Urban/Rural Context, Arkansas, 1865–1905* (Fayetteville: University of Arkansas Press, 1990), 62–63.

33. David Y. Thomas, ed., *Arkansas and Its People: A History, 1541–1930*, vol. 2 (New York: American Historical Society, 1930), 499.

34. Raymond Arsenault, *The Wild Ass of the Ozarks: Jeff Davis and the Social Bases of Southern Politics* (Philadelphia: Temple University Press, 1984), 205.

35. Ibid., 206.

36. Ibid., 207.

37. Marion Ingham to Orval Faubus, March 5, 1959, Orval Faubus Papers, box 301, file 11, Special Collections, University of Arkansas Libraries at Fayetteville.

38. Luville Milton to Orval Faubus, March 8, 1959, Orval Faubus Papers, box 301, file 11, Special Collections, University of Arkansas Libraries at Fayetteville.

39. Walter M. Ebel to Orval Faubus, Orval Faubus Papers, box 301, file 12, Special Collections, University of Arkansas Libraries at Fayetteville.

40. Grif Stockley, "The Twenty-one Deaths Caused by the 1959 Fire at the Negro Boys Industrial School: An Isolated Case of 'Neglect' or an Instance of Racial Violence?," in *Race and Ethnicity in Arkansas: New Perspectives*, ed. John A. Kirk, 71–81 (Fayetteville: University of Arkansas Press, 2014).

Chapter Two: The Second Most Powerful Governor

1. *Arkansas Democrat*, March 5, 1959.

2. Mack Sturgis to Orval Faubus, January 10, 1958, Orval Faubus Papers, box 301, file 16, University of Arkansas Libraries at Fayetteville.

3. Acts of Arkansas, 310 (1955), 1366–67; Ibid., 511 (1953), 645.

4. *Arkansas Democrat*, December 28, 1959.

5. Ibid.

6. A *New York Times* "notable book" selection in 1997, Roy Reed's biography of Orval Faubus is definitive. In addition, my present understanding of Orval Faubus has been enriched by conversations with Reed, and I have relied heavily on his book for details and insight into the governor's past.

7. The parallels between Faubus and Jeff Davis, who in his three two-years terms as governor (1901–1907) took genuine pleasure in baiting the citified sissies in Little Rock and their defender, the *Arkansas Gazette*, are too obvious to dismiss. Reed notes that Faubus actually saw himself as "a modern somewhat subtler version of Jeff Davis." Reed, *Faubus*, 132.

8. Daisy Bates, *The Long Shadow of Little Rock* (New York: David McKay, 1962), 55.

9. Quoted in Stockley, *Ruled by Race*, 116.

10. Quoted in Reed, *Faubus*, 219.

11. Reed points out that Faubus was mystified that others didn't think of politics so glibly.

12. Elizabeth Jacoway, *Turn Away Thy Son: Little Rock, the Crisis That Shocked the Nation* (New York: Free Press, 2007), 168.

13. Virginia was the only other state to try to close some of its schools to avoid integration. For a detailed description of the difficulties caused by the closures in Little Rock, see Sondra Gordy, *Finding the Lost Year: What Happened When Little Rock Closed Its Public Schools* ((Fayetteville, University of Arkansas Press, 2009), 2.

14. Named initially the Little Rock Private School Corporation, in honor of its founder, the school became the Raney Rebels in December.

15. *Arkansas Democrat*, March 5, 1959.

16. Ibid.

17. *Arkansas Gazette*, March 10, 1959.

18. Ibid., March 6, 1959.

19. Ibid., January 14, 1959.

20. *Arkansas Democrat*, March 5, 1959.

21. Ibid.

22. Ibid.

23. *Arkansas Gazette*, March 7, 1959.

24. *Arkansas Democrat*, March 5, 1959.

25. Story L. Matkin-Rawn, "'We Fight for the Rights of Our Race': Black Arkansans in the Era of Jim Crow" (PhD diss., University of Wisconsin at Madison, June 8, 2009), 174.

26. Jeannie Whayne, *Delta Empire: Lee Wilson and the Transformation of Agriculture in the New South* (Baton Rouge: Louisiana State University Press, 2011), 114.

27. Reed, *Faubus*, 257.

Chapter Three: Explaining the Fire

1. *Arkansas Democrat*, March 5, 1959.

2. Ibid.

3. Engel's name appears on the state's letterhead during this era.

4. *Arkansas Democrat*, March 5, 1959.

5. John Ward, interview by Grif Stockley, Little Rock, January 17. 2009, Grif Stockley Papers (location to be determined).

6. *Arkansas Gazette*, March 6, 1959.

7. Ibid.

8. Ibid.

9. *Arkansas Democrat*, March 6, 1959.

10. *Arkansas Gazette*, March 7, 1959.

11. The 1930 Census lists Lester and Mary Gaines as living at the Negro Boys Industrial School.

12. Eloise Coggs, interview by Grif Stockley, August 7, 2010, 7, Grif Stockley Papers.

13. Dr. Louis Coggs to Orval Faubus, March 6, 1959, Orval Faubus Papers, Box 301, File 21, Special Collections, University of Arkansas Libraries at Fayetteville.

14. David Y. Thomas, ed., *Arkansas and Its People, A History, 1541–1930*, vol. 2 (New York: American Historical Society, 1930), 503–4.

15. *Arkansas Gazette*, November 9, 1964.

16. Eloise Coggs, interview by Grif Stockley, August 7, 2010, 13. "So this guy, who comes out of Arkansas . . . he was Ricks. Ricks comes and he marries the Coggs girl. . . . And as a part of the dowry, he demanded twenty families. Twenty slave families. Which was my my [sic] grandfather was one of those families."

17. Eula Hopkins and Wanda Gray, eds., *History of Crawford County, Arkansas* (Van Buren, AR: Historical Preservation of Crawford County, 2001), 282.

18. George Lankford, *Bearing Witness: Memories of Arkansas Slavery* (Fayetteville: University of Arkansas Press, 2003), 67.

19. Ibid., 68.

20. Historians have learned that that Catcher was a town like a number of others in Arkansas in which whites forced the black population to leave their homes. Called Sundown Towns because in some communities blacks were explicitly warned to be out of town by the time the sun went down, the phenomenon of racial cleansing in the United States has not been limited to the South but has occurred all over the country. This phenomenon in Arkansas has been recently documented by a number of historians. See Guy Lancaster, *Racial Cleansing in Arkansas, 1883–1924: Politics, Land, Labor, and Criminality* (Lanham, MD: Lexington Books, 2014), 103–9; Guy Lancaster, "Racial Cleansing in the Arkansas Delta," in *Race and Ethnicity in Arkansas: New Perspectives*, ed. John A. Kirk, 49–59 (Fayetteville: University of Arkansas Press, 2014). For a national perspective, see James W. Loewen, *Sundown Towns: A Hidden Dimension of American Racism* (New York: The New Press, 2005). Since the last quarter of the twentieth century, there has been enormous interest in exploring Arkansas racial history. See Grif Stockley, *Ruled by Race: Black/White Relations in Arkansas from Slavery to the Present* (Fayetteville: University of Arkansas Press, 2009). With the advent of digital technology, the online Arkansas Encyclopedia of History and Culture has become a starting point for research in this area. An exhaustive bibliography can be found in Dr. Guy Lancaster's *Racial Cleansing in Arkansas* (2014), 143–50.

21. Wanda Gray, e-mail message to Grif Stockley, June 18, 2010. Historian Wanda Gray has documented that "Tandy Coggs paid the sum of $180 to Lewis

Bryan and his wife, Fannie for the NW Quarter of the Southwest Quarter of Section 3, Township 7 North, Range 31." The deed was filed at the Crawford County Circuit Clerk's office on November 13, 1883. Grif Stockley Papers.

22. *Arkansas Democrat*, August 12, 1951, Negroes Clipping File, Little Rock Library.

23. A variant on this story was told by granddaughter Eloise, who said in a 2010 interview that her father, Tandy Washington, "ran off without his father knowing and went to hear Dr. Booker speak.... And then he comes back and tells his father that he wants to go to [Arkansas] Baptist College where Dr. Booker is." Given his father's hopes for his son, it seems likely that Tandy Calvin would have gladly given his permission. In any event, Booker inspired him, and he was more determined than ever to get more education.

24. Arkansas Baptist College, http://www.encyclopediaofarkansas.net/encyclo pedia/entry-detail.aspx?entryID-2440.

25. Eloise Coggs, interview by Grif Stockley, August 7, 2010, 8. According to Eloise Coggs, her father's sister, Elizabeth Williams, graduated from Arkansas Baptist in 1912. In 1895 Booker T. Washington had advised American blacks not to worry about politics for the time being and to concentrate on building up the "race" through the creation of wealth by hard work. Grif Stockley Papers.

26. Frederick Chambers, "Historical Study of Arkansas Agricultural, Mechanical, and Normal College, 1873–1943." (EdD diss., Ball State University, 1970), 235n428.

27. Quoted in Story L. Matkin-Rawn, "'We Fight for the Rights of Our Race': Black Arkansans in the Era of Jim Crow" (PhD diss., University of Wisconsin at Madison, 2009), 184.

28. Chambers, "Historical Study," 234.

29. Eloise Coggs, interview by Grif Stockley. August 7, 2010.

30. After a dormitory was destroyed by fire, superintendent Tandy Washington Coggs ran the Negro Boys Industrial School in two locations south of Pine Bluff in the Jefferson County communities of Moscow and Tamo.

31. Eloise Coggs, interview by Grif Stockley, August 7, 2010, 10.

32. Ibid., 28–29.

33. Granville Coggs, interview by Grif Stockley, August 6, 2010, 13.

34. Ibid., Aug. 6, 2010.

35. Ibid.

36. *Arkansas Gazette*, December 16, 1930.

37. Eighth Biennial Report, Arkansas Boys' Industrial School (1934), Arkansas Studies Institute, Little Rock.

38. Quoted in Stockley, *Ruled by Race*, 220; Michael Dougan, *Arkansas Odyssey: The Saga of Arkansas from Prehistoric Times to Present* (Little Rock: Rose Publishing, 1994), 433.

39. Quoted in Stockley, *Ruled by Race*, 290; Eleventh Biennial Report, Arkansas Boys' Industrial School" (1940), Arkansas Studies Institute, Little Rock.

40. G. Back Papers, file 35, Arkansas Studies Institute, Little Rock.

Chapter Four: White Supremacy

1. *Pine Bluff Commercial*, April 18, 1937. Even after all this time, it is an article of faith among Coggs family members that the all-white board which oversaw both institutions (both white and black reform schools) was removed by Governor Carl Bailey en masse because it wouldn't fire Tandy Washington Coggs. In fact, the *Arkansas Democrat* on April 18, 1937, reported that Bailey "ousted" two members of the board "for their refusal to discharge John Reeves as superintendent [of the white boys' school]." A third member, Laura Fitzhugh, "mother of Thomas Fitzhugh, the governor's campaign manager" during the previous Democratic primary in August 1936, quit the board in protest after John Reeves turned in his forced resignation to the governor. Just two weeks earlier, she had made the nomination that resulted in the election of Reeves as superintendent by a 4 to 1 vote.

2. Stockley, *Ruled by Race*, 288.

3. Granville Coggs, interview by Grif Stockley, August 5, 2010, Grif Stockley Papers (location to be determined).

4. Betty Hood, interview by Grif Stockley, May 28, 2010, Grif Stockley Papers.

5. Octavia Hill, interview by Grif Stockley, December 1, 2011, Grif Stockley Papers.

6. Stockley, *Ruled by Race*, 230.

7. "Ben Laney Scrapbooks," vol. 5, *Hope Star*, August 3, 1945, M99–15 Ben T. Laney Collection, University of Central Arkansas Archives, Conway.

8. "Ben Laney Scrapbooks," vol. 6, *Arkansas Democrat*, August 22, 1945, M99–15 Ben T. Laney Collection, University of Central Arkansas Archives, Conway.

9. *State Press*, September 12, 1947.

10. "Ben Laney Scrapbooks," vol. 5, *Arkansas Gazette*, July 17, July 18, 1945, M99–15, Ben T. Laney Collection, University of Central Arkansas Archives, Conway.

11. "Ben Laney Scrapbooks," vol. 5, *El Dorado Evening Times*, August 4, 1945, M99–15 Ben T. Laney Collection, University of Central Arkansas Archives, Conway.

12. "Ben Laney Scrapbooks," vol. 5, *El Dorado Evening Times*, August 4, 1945, M99–15 Ben T. Laney Collection, University of Central Arkansas Archives.

13. "Ben Laney Scrapbooks," vol. 5, *Hope Star*, February 27, 1945, M99–15 Ben T. Laney Collection, University of Central Arkansas Archives..

14. "Ben Laney Scrapbooks," vol. 4, *Mena Evening Star*, February 16, 1945, M99–15 Ben T. Laney Collection, University of Central Arkansas Archives.

15. "McCuistion battled for funding for black schools." See Tom W. Dillard, "Ed McCuistion," *Arkansas Democrat-Gazette*, June 6, 2004, Grif Stockley Papers.

16. *Arkansas Gazette*, March 27, 1959.

17. The suits were against school boards in different parts of the state. Stephen A. Stephen, "Changes in the Status of Negroes in Arkansas, 1948–50," *Arkansas Historical Quarterly* 10 (Spring, 1951): 45.

18. Harry S. Ashmore, *Epitaph for Dixie* (New York: W. W. Norton, 1957), 56, 181.

19. Bureau of Labor Statistics, http:www.bls.gov/data/inflation_calculator.htm. Allowing for inflation in 2015 dollars, the amount diverted from black schools was $41,797,603.73.

20. *Arkansas Gazette*, April 5, 1949.

21. James T. Baker, *Brooks Hays* (Macon, GA: Mercer University Press, 1989), 142.

22. *Arkansas Gazette*, April 5, 1949.

23. Brooks Hays would wrestle with his conscience and religion and his desire for political power much of his life, and if he almost always came down on the side of his career when it came to civil rights, he would have the integrity finally to acknowledge it after he retired.

24. Stockley, *Ruled by Race*, 246, quoting John A. Kirk, *Redefining the Color Line: Black Activism in Little Rock, Arkansas 1940–1970* (Gainesville: University Press of Florida, 2002), 31.

25. *Arkansas Gazette*, April 13, 1949. Under an editorial titled "Are Words Enough?," Ashmore noted that the proposal "was a commendable statement, but it provides no positive answer to the problem created when local school districts divert to white schools thousands of dollars of state money appropriated for Negro education."

26. See Sidney S. McMath, *Promises Kept, A Memoir* (Fayetteville: University of Arkansas Press, 2003), 199, 200; James E. Lester, *A Man for Arkansas: Sid McMath and the Southern Reform Tradition* (Little Rock: Rose Publishing Company 1976).

27. *Report of Committee for State Training Schools*, March 26, 1952, Francis Cherry Papers, box 1, folder 59. Arkansas State Archives, Little Rock. Though this report was made during the last year of the McMath administration, the Cherry administration included it with other documents referenced in Chapter Five relating to the Negro Boys Industrial School.

28. Ed McCuistion, quoted in Francis Cherry Papers, box 1, folder 59, Arkansas State Archives, Little Rock; *Report of Five Person Committee for Study of State Training Schools*, March 26, 1952; Grif Stockley, "Twenty-one Deaths," in *Race and Ethnicity in Arkansas: New Perspectives*, ed. John A. Kirk (Fayetteville: University of Arkansas Press, 2014), 75. McCuistion's comments that the boys might do better if they were not institutionalized were worth remembering even after the fire. In

1962 tuberculosis would become a problem at NBIS. See J. H. Bates, W. E. Potts, and M. Lewis, M. "The Epidemiology of Primary Tuberculosis in an Industrial School," *New England Journal of Medicine* (1965); 272–714.

29. Ibid.

30. Ibid.

31. Ibid.

32. Ibid.

33. Ibid.

34. Ibid.

35. Ibid.

Chapter Five: How Things Work

1. Cynthia Rushing, interview by Grif Stockley, March 19, 2010, 1–5, Grif Stockley Papers (location to be determined).

2. Senator Ellis Fagan to Francis Cherry, February. 2, 1953, Francis Adams Cherry Papers, box 37, folder 229, Archives and Special Collections, Dean B. Ellis Library, Arkansas State University, Jonesboro.

3. Though he is remembered by many as a leader in the African American community, there were serious allegations that he was a tool of Little Rock business interests. See Stockley, *Ruled by Race*, 408–9.

4. Francis Adams Cherry Papers, Committee Findings at the Wrightsville Boys' Industrial School, box 37, folder 229, Archives and Special Collection, Dean B. Ellis Library, Arkansas State University, Jonesboro.

5. Charles Bussey to Francis Cherry, February 11, 1953, box 37, folder 229, Archives and Special Collection, Dean B. Ellis Library, Arkansas State University, Jonesboro.

6. Act 511 of 1953.

7. Gordon Morgan, "The Arkansas Negro Boys Institution and Organization" (master's thesis, University of Arkansas, 1956).

8. A. J. Moss to Francis Cherry, June 20, 1953, box 1, folder 58, Francis A. Cherry Papers, Arkansas State Archives, Little Rock.

9. Both reports spelled his name "Rollins."

10. Ella Mae Rawlings, interview by Jajuan Johnson, Butler Center for Arkansas Studies, Little Rock. AV Project. http://arstudies.contentdm.oclc.org/cdm/search/collection/p1532coll1/searchterm/ella/order/title.

11. Ken Francis to D. E. Blackmon. August 25, 1953, box 1, folder 58, Francis A. Cherry Papers, box 1, folder 58, Arkansas State Archives, Little Rock.

12. Ibid.

13. Grif Stockley, *Daisy Bates: Civil Rights Crusader from Arkansas* (Jackson: University Press of Mississippi, 2005), 52, quoting Daisy Bates, interview by Elizabeth Jacoway, October 11, 1976, 5, Southern Oral History Program, Library of North Carolina at Chapel Hill.

14. April 12, 1955 minutes, Negro Boys Industrial School, box 301, file 16, Orval Faubus Papers, Special Collections, University of Arkansas Libraries at Fayetteville.

15. May 17, 1955 minutes, Negro Boys Industrial School, box 301, file 16, Orval Faubus Papers, Special Collections. University of Arkansas Libraries at Fayetteville.

16. Morgan, "Arkansas Negro Boys Institution," 44

17. Ibid., 42

18. Ibid., 67.

19. Ibid., 28.

20. Ibid.

21. The problem of accounting for revenue extended into the 1960s.

22. Morgan, "Arkansas Negro Boys Institution," 33

23. Ibid., 62.

24. Barbara Gatlin, telephone interview by Grif Stockley, June 6, 2009, notes of author, Grif Stockley Papers.

25. Clara Gerard to Orval Faubus, Orval Faubus Papers, Special Collections, University of Arkansas Libraries at Fayetteville.

26. Though Wrightsville was at the time an unincorporated farming community of roughly one thousand mostly black residents with no running water, it could boast that it had a high school with twelve grades. J. C. Cook, a successful black farmer, donated the land for what would become J. C. Cook High School and became the school's principal and the postmaster of Wrightsville. J. C. Cook High School is best known to historians of the Central High School Crisis as one of two black high schools in Pulaski County that accepted many more students than it could comfortably accommodate during the Lost Year. Goforth Coleman, a well-known advocate for racial justice who would become the last executive director of the Arkansas Council on Human Relations, remembered the J. C. Cook school as having more than forty students in a classroom. He told historian Sondra Gordy that "we were still able to get . . . I won't say a quality education but I think we were able to continue the process." As in many towns in Arkansas, Wrightsville's commercial establishments were dominated by whites in this era. Two residents, who still live in Wrightsville, could name three other businesses owned by whites besides the Gerards. In a letter to the author, the former mayor of Wrightsville, Lorraine Smith, the daughter of J. C. Cook, remembered attending church in Little Rock with Lester and Mary Gaines, calling them "very respectable people." She, too, had graduated from Arkansas AM&N.

Chapter Six: Not Business as Usual

1. Grif Stockley, *Blood in their Eyes: The Elaine Race Massacres of 1919* (Fayetteville: University of Arkansas Press, 2001.

2. Grif Stockley, *Ruled by Race: Black/White Relations in Arkansas from Slavery to the Present* (Fayetteville: University of Arkansas Press, 2008), 359–66

3. John A. Kirk, "The Killing of Carnell Russ: Civil Rights, Law Enforcement, and the Courts," *Arkansas Historical Quarterly* 74 (Autumn 2015): 231–56. Kirk painstakingly traces the trials and appeals by the family for nine years that came to nothing. For those who were willing to confront this aspect of white supremacy directly in all its savagery, L. C. Bates between 1941 and 1959 documented its brutality of with accounts of beatings of blacks that occurred in central Arkansas and also in towns primarily in Delta counties and in the southern part of the state. In the pages of the *State Press* for October 9, 1942, one learns about a black minister named Thomas Palmer in North Little Rock who was "brutally beaten by a group of white men" and interrogated: "What kind of meetings have you attended lately? There had been some northern Negroes down here putting things in you Southern niggers head."

4. "Confidential Investigation," Orval Faubus Papers, box 302, file 12, University of Arkansas Libraries at Fayetteville.

5. Ibid., 4.

6. Ibid., 10.

7. Ibid., 12.

8. Mabel Fleming, interview by Grif Stockley and Frank Lawrence, June 5, 2010, Grif Stockley Papers (location to be determined).

9. "Confidential Investigation," Orval Faubus Papers, box 302, file 12, 13, University of Arkansas Libraries at Fayetteville.

10. Ibid., 15.

11. Ibid., 19.

12. Ibid., 21.

13. Ibid., 23.

14. Ibid., 25.

15. Ibid.

16. Legislative subcommittee report, 11/28/1958, 4, Grif Stockley Papers.

17. Dorothy Mattison, interview by Grif Stockley, January 27, 2010, Grif Stockley Papers.

Chapter Seven: Us versus Them

1. *Arkansas Democrat*, March 10, 2013.

2. *Arkansas Gazette*, March 15, 1959.

3. Carmen Ruthling to Orval Faubus, March 6, 1959, Orval Faubus Papers, box 302, folder 11, Special Collections, University of Arkansas Libraries at Fayetteville.

4. Charles Austin to Orval Faubus, March 6, 1959, and A. H. Hill to Orval Faubus, March 8, 1959; ibid.

5. Orval Faubus to Rev. Jacob C. Oglesby, Orval Faubus Papers, box 301, file 21, Special Collections, University of Arkansas Libraries at Fayetteville.

6. Virgil Blossom, *It HAS Happened Here* (New York: Harper, 1959), 137.

7. Reed, *Faubus*, 260.

8. Numan V. Bartley, *The Rise of Massive Resistance: Race and Politics in the South during the 1950's* (Baton Rouge: Louisiana State University Press, 1969), 3.

9. Sue McKenzie (Arkansas Department of Education), e-mail message to Marge Roberts (February 3, 2009): "I believe the Board did approve the textbooks in 1958 as they do now," Grif Stockley Papers (location to be determined).

10. Walter L. Brown, *Our Arkansas* (Austin, TX: The Steck Company, 1958), 18. As an admirer of Dr. Brown and the winner of the Walter L. Brown Award for "best article published in a county or local historical journal in 2008 . . . for [my] article 'The Negro Boys Industrial School Fire: A Holistic Approach to History,'" I wrote a letter to him while researching this book and recited the quotation above and asked the following question: "Obviously, if you were writing the same book today, it would begin much differently. I wanted to give you the opportunity to respond." For whatever reason, Dr. Brown did not respond to my letter. Grif Stockley to Dr. Walter Brown, February 1, 2010. On September 23, 2011, I followed up with another letter to Dr. Brown but it was returned "refused." Grif Stockley Papers. I would later be informed that Dr. Brown was suffering from dementia.

11. Brown, *Our Arkansas*, 214, 265.

12. Ruth Suddeth, Isa Lloyd Osterhout, and George Lewis Hutcheson, *Empire Builders of Georgia* (Austin, TX: The Steck Company, 1957), 186–87. "The plantation force of workers has been likened to a conscript army living in barracks. The master was captain, the overseer, lieutenant, and the slaves themselves were privates. . . . In general, where the master lived on the plantation, there was a happy relationship between him and his slaves." As has been acknowledged by many others, the bitterness between the South and the rest of country over the Civil War was consciously laid to rest not only by politicians but by textbook writers. In the preface to the ninth printing of the college text, *A Short History of the American People*, vol. 1, *1492–1865* (Toronto: D. Van Nostrand, 1949), authors Oliver Chitwood and Frank Owsley advise their readers that certain historical issues are simply too

delicate to discuss: "We have, however, made a strenuous effort to suspend our political and sectional prejudices and even our patriotism while discussing international disputes and the controversies that led to the Civil War. We have left it to the reader to evaluate the ethics of these conflicts and have made no effort to apportion praise or blame to the contestants. Indeed, we do not feel that in any of these controversies one side was altogether right and the other altogether wrong."

13. Compare Hazel Presson and David Y. Thomas, *The Story of Arkansas* (Little Rock: Little Rock Democrat Printing and Lithographing Co., 1942), 230. "Sometimes the ghosts asked for a drink of water, gulping down a bucketful at a time! They did this by pouring the water into a bucket under their robes." "Asking the Negroes for water, each would apparently drink a bucketful. The water was really emptied into water bags hidden under their robes," Brown, *Our Arkansas*, 212.

14. Brown, *Our Arkansas*, 192.

15. Quoted in Carl H. Moneyhon, *The Impact of the Civil War and Reconstruction on Arkansas: Persistence in the Midst of Ruin* (Little Rock: Little Rock Democrat Printing and Lithographing Co., 1942), 140.

16. For a summary of citations, see Grif Stockley, *Ruled by Race: Black/White Relations in Arkansas from Slavery to the Present* (Fayetteville: University of Arkansas Press, 2008), 467n17.

17. Brown, Our Arkansas, 192.

18. Ibid., 211.

19. Ibid., 209

20. Ibid., 100, 101.

21. Ibid., 4.

22. The plaque reads, "Walter L. Brown was an esteemed member of the University of Arkansas faculty from 1954 to 1990. Known for his inspired teaching, he instilled in his students a love of learning that lasted far beyond the time they spent on campus. He also secured the university's reputation as the state's flagship institution for Arkansas studies. For more than thirty years, he promoted the study of Arkansas history as a professor, editor of the *Arkansas Historical Quarterly* (1959–1990), and secretary-treasurer of the Arkansas Historical Association (1955–1990). Dr. Brown made the *Arkansas Historical Quarterly* a scholarly journal, ensuring that it kept abreast of new interests and methodologies in history while never wavering in its devotion to Arkansas and its people. Under his leadership, the quarterly published some of the earliest scholarship on Arkansas's African American and civil rights history. A respected scholar himself, Brown wrote the definitive biography of Albert Pike, a colorful figure of central importance to the politics and culture of antebellum and Civil War–era Arkansas, as well as a widely used children's textbook."

23. The three editions of *Our Arkansas* are archived at the Butler Center for Arkansas Studies in Little Rock. On February 9, 2015, at the Butler Center for

Arkansas Studies, archival assistant Nathania Sawyer and the author compared the content of the three editions and found almost no differences, including the number of pages.

24. Margaret Smith Ross, "Have We Neglected Negro History?," *Pulaski County Historical Review* 1–IV (March 1956): 12–14.

25. Ibid.

26. *The Nation*, December 27, 1933, 734.

27. John Gould Fletcher, *Arkansas* (Chapel Hill: University of North Carolina Press, 1947), 79.

28. Ibid., 89

29. Ben F. Johnson III, *Fierce Solitude: A Life of John Gould Fletcher* (Fayetteville: University of Arkansas Press, 1994), 245.

30. Fletcher, *Arkansas*, 842.

31. Orville W. Taylor, *Negro Slavery in Arkansas*, Reprint (1958; repr., Fayetteville: University Press of Arkansas, 2000), quoting from the introduction by Professor Carl H. Moneyhon at xiv.

32. Taylor's book references only three of the "slave narratives," the interviews conducted by the writers for the Federal Writers Project in the 1930s and those only secondarily. As it so happened, Arkansas interviewers, particularly African American S. S. Taylor, who went on to become the associate editor at the *State Press*, were considered some of the best interviewers employed by the Works Progress Administration.

33. In fairness, as previously mentioned, the Arkansas History Commission was devoid of primary materials about African Americans. Additionally, the Slave Narratives containing interviews from all the former Confederate states at that time were not indexed by state.

34. Blake Wintory, "William Hines Furbush, African-American Carpetbagger, Republican, Fusionist and Democrat," *Arkansas Historical Quarterly* 63 (Summer 2004): 61–107.

Chapter Eight: Hanging Together

1. *Arkansas Democrat*, March 25, 1959.

2. Orval Faubus to Parent, Orval Faubus Papers, box 311, folder 20, University of Arkansas Libraries at Fayetteville.

3. James Sherman Watson, interview by Grif Stockley, September 14, 2011, Grif Stockley Papers (location to be determined). Mr. Watson, who had been diagnosed with cancer, sat through the interview with his daughter and his spouse, Ollie Watson, at the Garland County Library in Hot Springs.

4. *Arkansas Democrat*, April 17, 1959.

5. *Arkansas Gazette*, March 26, 1959.

6. Ibid.

7. J. C. Hawkins to Orval Faubus, March 24, 1959, Orval E. Faubus Papers, box 301, file 11, University of Arkansas Libraries at Fayetteville. In the upper right corner of the letter are the words, "Confidential File Negro School."

8. *State Press*, March 27, 1942.

9. Grif Stockley, *Daisy Bates: Civil Rights Crusader from Arkansas* (Jackson: University Press of Mississippi, 2005), 265, quoting L. C. Bates in *Arkansas Gazette*, January 22, 1972.

10. *State Press*, April 3, 1959; Irene Wassell, "L.C. Bates, Editor of the *Arkansas State Press*" (master's thesis, University of Arkansas at Little Rock, 1983). The most detailed interview given by L. C. Bates about his past was his interview with Wassell.

11. The reference of a past arrangement with "Buddy Hackett" is mentioned here because of T. J. Raney's close relationship with Orval Faubus and his financial dealings with the Wrightsville institution. As noted previously, Raney rented acreage not in cultivation from the Wrightsville institution. The board was aware that the boys were being used as day labor. I have not been able to locate the minutes of the board meeting in which the actual arrangement was discussed, but Frank Lawrence has suggested that "Inmates were Illegally Used to Work Fields. Alfred Smith and L.R. Gaines Get $1 Per Day for Each Boy's Labor." Frank Lawrence File, Grif Stockley Papers. I found no evidence pro or con that either Alfred Smith and/or Lester Gaines raked off a percentage for themselves. At the same time, it is unclear whether accounting procedures were set up to show how this money was dispersed. As I discuss in the final chapter, by 1961 this practice appeared to trouble the legislative audit committee.

12. Minutes of the April 1, 1959 Board Meeting of the NBIS, Orval Faubus Papers, box 301, file 20, University of Arkansas Libraries, Fayetteville. E-mail message from University archivist Geoffery Stark to Grif Stockley January 17, 2008, summarizing in part the actions of the board: "The April 1, 1959 minutes in box 301, folder 20, contains Mr. Gaines's resignation before the board. Afterward, the staff requested to address the board and also resigned, though they agreed to stay on until they could be replaced." Grif Stockley Papers.

13. *Arkansas Democrat*, April 2, 1959. Accounts of the dismissal of the employees were carried in several out-of-state newspapers such as the *Chicago Defender* as well as the *Arkansas Gazette* and the *State Press*.

14. Report from the Arkansas Criminal Investigation Division (CID) concerning communications with NBIS board members J. C. Hawkins and Alfred Smith on the night of April 3, 1959. Orval Faubus Papers, box 301, folder 12, University of Arkansas Libraries, Fayetteville.

15. Additional report from State Police concerning incident on April 3, 1959, Orval Faubus Papers, box 301, folder 20, University of Arkansas Libraries, Fayetteville.

16. *Arkansas Democrat*, April 17, 1959. According to personnel in the auditing division of the legislature, audits for this era no longer exist.

17. Orval Faubus to Louis Coggs, March 6, 1959, Orval Faubus Papers, box 301, file 21, University of Arkansas Libraries, Fayetteville.

18. Christopher Mercer, e-mail message to Grif Stockley, June 3, 2010, Grif Stockley Papers.

19. Under Arkansas law, as in other jurisdictions, individuals who are harmed by actions attributable to the state may seek monetary damages through an administrative procedure. By design, the procedure is not considered a legal action in order to avoid the defense that an individual may not sue the state.

20. State Claims Commission Docket, Claim No. 59–27-CC Willie Piggee, Adminstrator of the Estate of William Loyd Piggee, Claimant vs. Negro Boys Industrial School, State, Arkansas Respondent.

21. *In the Matter of the Estate of Lindsey Cross*, in the Probate Court of Pulaski County, Arkansas No. 34802, Order Appointing Administrator, No. 34802.

22. State Claims Commission Docket, Claim No. 59–26-CC W.J. Walker, Adminstrator of the Estate of Lindsey Cross, Claimant v. Negro Boys Industrial School, State of Arkansas, Respondent.

23. *In the Matter of the Estate of Lindsey Cross,* Probate Court of Pulaski County No. 34802, Petition for Appointment of Adminstrator.

24. Arkansas State Claims Commission Docket, Claim No. 59–34-CC Rebecca Nelson, Administratrix of the Estate of Johnnie Tillison, Deceased v. Negro Boys Industrial School, 11

25. In the interest of full disclosure, Phillip McMath, an attorney in his deceased father's firm, is a personal friend of the author. I asked him to read a draft of the above chapter to get his comments. He responded by e-mail on September 13, 2011. I have summarized his comments as follows:

Mr. McMath acknowledged that at my request, he had read the chapter on the manuscript that involved the McMath firm but was only about fourteen years old and has almost no memory of any of the events in this chapter. He has personal knowledge that it was not at all usual for his father or his father's partner, Henry Woods, to charge an attorney's fee of 40 percent. More typically, their fee was one-third in addition to costs. According to Mr. McMath, the explanation for this unusual fee may have to do with attorney Carl Langston, who was not a member of the firm but appears to have associated the McMath firm, which would mean that he received 20 percent and the McMath firm 20 percent and which explains the 40 percent figure. Mr. McMath said he had seen that kind of arrangement. As to the figure of 50 percent, which was the attorney's fee of 50 percent listed in the final order signed by the judge, he had no knowledge of why that arrangement was made. He said that he knew that neither his father nor his partner Henry Wood ever charged a 50 percent fee. Responding to my comment that Ms. Cross would have been better off without an attorney, he said he doubted if Ms. Cross would have received anything at all if she had represented herself because of racism and the difficult legal and factual questions.

26. As mentioned in the first chapter my notes from interviews with Ms. Long and family members are in Grif Stockley Papers.

Chapter Nine: Grand Jury

1. Ernest Dumas, e-mail message to Grif Stockley, July 29, 2011, Grif Stockley Papers (location to be determined).

2. Grif Stockley, *Ruled by Race: Black/White Relations in Arkansas from Slavery to the Present* (Fayetteville: University of Arkansas Press, 2008), 359. "Warned by the federal judge in open court that the Grand Jury could not withstand a legal challenge, the members of the Grand Jury met no more [to investigate conditions at the County Farm]." Grif Stockley, *Blood in Their Eyes: The Elaine Race Massacres of 1919* (Fayetteville: University of Arkansas Press, 2001).

Convictions of six of the black defendants in the Elaine Race Massacres were reversed by the Arkansas Supreme Court after defense attorneys were able to preserve for appeal a challenge to the composition of the grand jury and petit jury.

3. B. Finley Vinson, interviewed by John Kirk, February 25, 1993, 17, 18, John A. Kirk Interview Project, Pryor Center for Arkansas Oral and Visual History Project, University of Arkansas Libraries, Fayetteville.

4. Stockley, *Ruled by Race*, 316. COCA initially began meeting with the Little Rock City Board "as early as July 21, 1961" though it would take litigation to bring the city into compliance.

5. Vinson, interviewed by John Kirk, February 25, 1993, 9

6. *Arkansas Gazette*, March 7, 1960.

7. Stockley, *Ruled by Race*, 300–306

8. *Arkansas Gazette*, May 23, 1960

9. Ibid., April 22, 1961.

10. Stockley, *Ruled by Race*, 221.

11. *Arkansas Gazette*, April 22, 1961.

12. Howard Lee Nash, telephone interview by Grif Stockley, June 19, 2009.

13. Alvin Peters, interview by Frank Lawrence and Grif Stockley, March 2008, Grif Stockley Papers.

14. Stockley, *Ruled by Race*, 326, quoted in Nick Koltz, *Judgment Days: Lyndon Baines Johnson, Martin Luther King, Jr., and the Laws That Changed America* (New York: Houghton Mifflin, 2005), 153.

15. Roy Reed, *Faubus: The Life and Times of an American Prodigal* (Fayetteville: University of Arkansas Press, 1997), 265.

16. *Arkansas Gazette*, April 1, 1964.

17. Stockley, *Ruled by Race*, 340.

18. Board of Managers of the Arkansas Training School for Boys at Wrightsville v. George, 377 F.2d 228 (8th Cir. 1968).

Chapter Ten: Lessons Learned and Not Learned

1. Frank Lawrence, interview with Annette Himmelbaum, ca. October 15, 2008, Frank Lawrence File, Grif Stockley Papers (location to be determined).

2. Frank Lawrence, e-mail message to Grif Stockley, November 10, 2009, Grif Stockley Papers. "I do recall the elder Hall (large obese one) mentioning he knew his dad met with Faubus. In his words, this was the basis for them understanding how he lied about being in the outer hallway next to the stove the night of the fire. In fact Wilson Hall was not there at all. This was the impulse for Faubus to unleash the tirade primarily against L.R. Gaines. You are right, [Arthur] Hall then made no mention on camera and I didn't press the issue."

3. Dorothy Mattison, interview by Grif Stockley, January 27, 2010, Grif Stockley Papers.

4. Grif Stockley, *Ruled by Race: Black/White Relations in Arkansas from Slavery to the Present* (Fayetteville: University of Arkansas Press, 2008), 287, 289.

5. Orval Faubus, *Down from the Hills, II* (Little Rock: Democrat Printing and Lithographing Co., 1985), 17. "To me it was inadequate justice to the youths who burned to death as a result of negligence and dereliction of duty of those who were responsible for their care. Someone should have been prosecuted." Perhaps aware that some might wonder if the fire had been set intentionally by whites, he notes, "All employees at the school were black people." *Down from the Hills, I* and *II* were self-published and contain no endnotes or documentation. Knowing some of his actions during his six terms in office would continue to be judged harshly, his "histories" make no attempt to include any criticism of himself and constitute a highly selective version of significant events of his life and administrations. He would not live to see Roy Reed's fair treatment of him.

6. Roy Reed, *Faubus: The Life and Times of an American Prodigal* (Fayetteville: University of Arkansas Press, 1997), xii.

7. After reporting on politics for the *Arkansas Gazette* at the time of the fire, Reed was national and foreign correspondent for the *New York Times* from 1965 to 1978 before returning to teach journalism at the University of Arkansas, where he would become professor emeritus and publish his book on Faubus in 1997.

8. Orval Faubus to Rupert Hemphill, April 7, 1966, Orval Faubus Papers, box 302, file 10, University of Arkansas Libraries, Fayetteville.

9. Keith Lawrence and Terry Keleher, "Structural Racism and Community Change," The Aspen Institute Roundtable on Community Change, https://www.aspeninstitute.org/programs/roundtable-on-community-change.

10. Kwame Anthony Appiah, *The Honor Code: How Moral Revolutions Happen* (New York: Oxford University Press, 2011), xix.

11. See John A. Kirk, *Beyond Little Rock: The Origins and Legacies of the Central High Crisis* (Fayetteville: University of Arkansas Press, 2007).

12. Nat Griswold, "The Second Reconstruction in Little Rock," " unpublished MS (n.d.), Sara Alderman Murphy Papers, University of Arkansas Libraries, Fayetteville. For a more optimistic view of the work of the Arkansas Council on Human Relations, see John A. Kirk, 1954–1964, "Facilitating Change: The Arkansas Council on Human Relations, http://Plaza.UFL.edu.wardbkirk.doc. John A. Kirk, *Redefining the Color Line: Black Activism in Little Rock, 1940–1970* (Gainesville: University Press of Florida, 2002).

13. State of Arkansas Executive Department Proclamation, March 4, 2011, proclaiming March 5, 2011, as Arkansas Negro Boys Industrial School Fire Remembrance Day, Grif Stockley Papers.

14. In 2007 Congress had passed legislation popularly known as the Emmett Till Unsolved Civil Rights Crime Act and appropriated $100,000 to investigate unsolved civil rights violations.

15. Peggy Duncan, telephone interview by Grif Stockley, May 8, 2012, Grif Stockley Papers.

16. Ardecy and Archie Gyce, interview by Grif Stockley. April 6, 2014, Grif Stockley Papers.

17. The author's first meeting with Frank Lawrence was in February 2008 at the Butler Center for Arkansas Studies in Little Rock with Guy Lancaster (now Dr. Lancaster), who is editor of the online Encyclopedia of Arkansas History and Culture and Leslie Peacock of the weekly *Arkansas Times*. I should add that Leslie, who was researching a story about the fire, does not recall being present for this meeting.

18. Arkansas State Securities Office File, Grif Stockley Papers.

19. See, for example, Mary Hargrove, "Beat him up and do him good. Don't leave any marks," http://www.nospank.net/hargrove.htm. *Arkansas*

Democrat-Gazette, June 1998. The implementation of measures to racially integrate American society has most often fallen on the poor and uneducated in America. Michelle Alexander, *The New Jim Crow: Mass Incarceration in the Age of Color Blindness* (New York: The New Press 2010).

20. *Arkansas Gazette-Democrat*, November 4, 2015. On November 3, 2015, Baker Kurrus, superintendent of the Little Rock School District, told the weekly gathering of the Rotary Club that unless dramatic changes occurred, "If you like Detroit, you are going to love Little Rock. It's that simple." The devil was in the details. What changes needed to be made and who would make them are at the center of the debate.

Bibliography

Interviews

Coggs, Eloise, August 7, 2010.

Coggs, Granville, August 6, 2010.

Fleming, Mabel, June 5, 2010.

Hill, Octavia, December 1, 2011.

Hood, Betty, May 28, 2010.

Lawrence, Frank, July 17, 2008.

Lawrence, Greg, telephone calls, November 5, November 11, 2009.

Long, Luvenia, October 19, 2009.

Mattison, Dorothy, January 27, 2010.

Nash, Howard, telephone call, June 19, 2009.

Rushing, Cynthia, March 19, 2010.

Strickland, Josephine, telephone calls, November 10, 2009, January 16, 2010.

Ward, John, January 17, 2009.

Watson, James Sherman, September 14, 2011.

Archival Sources

UCA Archives. Ben Laney Collection. University of Central Arkansas, M99-15, Conway.

Francis Cherry Papers MS 0007, box 1, folders 58–61. Arkansas State Archives, Little Rock. Orval E. Faubus Papers. University of Arkansas Libraries Special Collections. David Mullins Library. University of Arkansas at Fayetteville.

Registration Ledger. Negro Boys Industrial School, 1930–1978. Grif Stockley Papers.

Newspapers

Arkansas Democrat

Arkansas Democrat-Gazette

Arkansas Gazette

Arkansas State Press
Arkansas Times
Chicago Defender
New York Times
Pine Bluff Commercial

Journal Articles and Book Chapters

Casey, Paula J. "Arkansas Juvenile Courts: Do Lay Judges Satisfy Due Process in Delinquency Cases?" 6 UALR L. Review 501 (1983).

Kirk, John. "Daisy Bates, the National Association for the Advancement of Colored People, and the Little Rock Central High Crisis: A Gendered Perspective." In *Gender and the Civil Rights Movement*, edited by Peter L. Ling and Sharon Monteith, 17–40. New York: Garland 1999

Ross, Margaret. "Have We Neglected Negro History?" *Pulaski County Historical Review.* (March 1956): 12–14.

Stockley, Grif. "The Negro Boys Industrial School Fire: A Holistic Approach to History," *Pulaski County Historical Review* 56 (Summer 2008): 39–54.

Stockley, Grif. "The Twenty-One Deaths Caused by the 1959 Fire at the Arkansas Negro Boys Industrial School: An Isolated Case of Neglect or an Instance of Racial Violence?" In *Race and Ethnicity in Arkansas New Perspectives*, edited by John A. Kirk, 71–81. Fayetteville: University of Arkansas Press, 2014.

Wintory, Blake. "William Hines Furbush African American Carpetbagger, Republican, Fusionist and Democrat." *Arkansas Historical Quarterly* 63 (Summer 2004): 107–61.

Books

Arsenault, Raymond. *The Wild Ass of the Ozarks: Jeff Davis and the Social Bases of Southern Politics* (Philadelphia: Temple University Press 1984).

Ashmore, Harry. *Epitaph for Dixie.* New York: W. W. Norton 1957.

Baker, James. T. *Brooks Hays.* Macon, GA: Mercer University Press, 1989.

Baldwin, James. *The Price of the Ticket: Collected Nonfiction 1948–1985.* New York: St. Martins/Marek, 1985.

Bartley, Numan. *The Rise of Massive Resistance: Race and Politics in the South during the 1950's.* Baton Rouge: Louisiana State University Press, 1969.

Bates, Daisy. *The Long Shadow of Little Rock*. New York: David McKay, 1962.

Blossom, Virgil. *It HAS Happened Here*. New York: Harper, 1959.

Bradburn, Cary. On the Opposite Shore: The Making of North Little Rock. Marceline, MO: Walsworth Printing, 2004.

Brown, Walter L. *Our Arkansas*. Austin, TX: The Steck Company, 1958.

Dougan, Michael. *Arkansas Odyssey: The Saga of Arkansas from Prehistoric Times to Present*. Little Rock, AR: Rose Publishing, 1994.

Fletcher, John Gould. *Arkansas*. Chapel Hill: University of North Carolina Press, 1947.

Goleman, Daniel. *Vital Lies, Simple Truths: The Psychology of Self-Deception*. New York: Simon and Schuster, 1985.

Gordy, Sondra. *Finding the Lost Year: What Happened When Little Rock Closed Its Public Schools*. Fayetteville: University of Arkansas Press, 2009.

Graves, John. *Town and Country: Race Relations and Urban Development in Arkansas, 1865–1905*. Fayetteville: University of Arkansas Press, 1996.

Hopkins, Eula, and Wanda Gray. *History of Crawford County*. Van Buren, AR: Historical Preservation of Crawford County, 2001.

Jacoway, Elizabeth. *Turn Away Thy Son: Little Rock, the Crisis That Shocked the Nation*. New York: Free Press, 2007.

Johnson, Ben III. *Fierce Solitude: A Life of John Gould Fletcher*. Fayetteville: University Press of Arkansas, 1994.

Lankford, George. *Bearing Witness: Memories of Arkansas Slavery*. Fayetteville: University of Arkansas Press, 2003.

Moneyhon, Carl H. *The Impact of the Civil War and Reconstruction on Arkansas: Persistence in the Midst of Ruin*. Little Rock, AR: Little Rock Democrat Printing and Lithographing, 1942.

Reed, Roy. *Faubus: The Life and Times of an American Prodigal*. Fayetteville: University of Arkansas Press, 1997.

Stockley, Grif. *Daisy Bates: Civil Rights Crusader from Arkansas*. Jackson: University Press of Mississippi, 2005.

Stockley, Grif. *Ruled by Race: Black/White Relations in Arkansas from Slavery to the Present*. Fayetteville: University of Arkansas Press, 2009.

Suddeth, Ruth, Isa Lloyd Osterhout, and George Lewis Hutcheson. *Empire Builders of Georgia*. Austin, TX: The Steck Company 1957.

Taylor, Orville W. *Negro Slavery in Arkansas*. 1958. Reprint, Fayetteville: University Press of Arkansas, 2000.

Thomas, David, ed. *Arkansas and Its People, A History*, vol. 2. New York: The American Historical Society, 1930.

Dissertations and Master's Thesis

Chambers, Frederick. "Historical Study of Arkansas Agricultural, Mechanical, and Normal College, 1873–1943." EdD diss., Ball State University, 1970.

Matkin-Rawn, Story L. "'We Fight for the Rights of Our Race': Black Arkansans in the Era of Jim Crow." PhD diss., University of Wisconsin at Madison, 2009.

Morgan, Gordon. "The Arkansas Negro Boys Institution and Organization." Master's thesis, University of Arkansas at Fayetteville, 1956.

Miscellaneous

Bureau of Labor Statistics, http:www.bls.gov/data/inflation_calculator.htm.

Butler Center for Arkansas Studies, Audio-Visual Project Interviews, Little Rock.

Eighth Biennial Report Arkansas Boys Industrial School, Phillip G. Back Papers, file 35, Arkansas Studies Institute, Little Rock.

Lawrence, Frank (copies of material contained in file of Frank Lawrence in the Grif Stockley Papers).

State Claims Commission Docket Claim No. 59–34-CC.

US Census. 1930.

Index

Printed in the United States
By Bookmasters